SONGS
FOR THE
JOURNEY
HOME

Songs for the Journey Home
Alchemy through Imagery—A Tarot Pathway

© Catherine Cook and Dwariko von Sommaruga, 1993
Alchemists & Artists
PO Box 32 305, Devonport, Auckland
New Zealand

ISBN 0 473 02134 X

Produced by Renée Lang

Designed by Suellen Allen
Text edited by Alison Dench
Typeset by Egan-Reid Ltd
Printed by GP Print

Accompanying tarot deck printed by Parnell Printers Ltd

Alchemy Through Imagery: A Tarot Pathway

S O N G S
F O R T H E
J O U R N E Y
H O M E

Catherine Cook and Dwariko von Sommaruga

ACKNOWLEDGEMENTS

Together we acknowledge the depth of our friendship, mutual respect and co-creativity which has led to the birth of the book and the cards. We have felt the presence of divine protection and guidance throughout this process of discovering our Songs for the Journey Home.

Many dear friends both in New Zealand and overseas have fed us with their enthusiasm. We now offer back this feast of images and words.

We have been blessed with tremendous support from: Elizabeth Beadman, who has sent waves of love, encouragement and belief in us over the Tasman Sea throughout the last four years; Hugh Cook, who inspired us through his creative discipline, giving generously of his time and resources, providing a computer and teaching the required wordprocessing skills; Cathie Dunsford, our editor, who has been the glorious catalyst we needed to bring about the final structure and form the book has taken.

Catherine:

My beloved partner Alan McDonald has radiated encouragement from the furnace of his Leonine heart. He has unreservedly recognised the hundreds of hours alone that I have required for writing and reflecting.

My heartfelt thanks to my parents, Patricia and Wally, who brought me gently into this lifetime. Their love created the safe harbour of my childhood. The inner world of my imagination was fuelled by the large portions of their time given over to storytelling and make-believe. My fantasy world was never squashed and this has allowed my visions to surface easily as an adult.

I want to express my appreciation to Lyndsay Rendall for the constancy and strength of her friendship and wise counsel.

Dwariko:

I am grateful to my parents, Lyndsay and Lorenz for a childhood imbued with drama, art, dance, music, swimming and boating. The strength of these foundations of aesthetic appreciation and my tremendous pleasure in the creative process have been fully re-awakened through creating the tarot deck.

I thank my daughters Sara and Emilie for their love and faith in me and their absolute delight as each image emerged.

CONTENTS

INTRODUCING

Songs for the Journey Home

*S*ongs for the Journey Home is a celebratory topographical mapping of the peaks and valleys which make up the integral landscape of human experiences. At times we are able to view the events of our lives from an elevated vantage point, seeing the 'big picture' and identifying both the pathways which have led us here and our future route. However, when we move down into the shady groves it is very easy to lose that sense of perspective and direction and become paralysed through fear of taking a wrong turning. This fear diminishes our instinctive knowing and rational decision-making processes.

The archetypal imagery of tarot shows us symbolically where we are. These images also awaken our recognition of the pertinence of all our encounters, so that we can move away from harshly judging our times in the valleys, through longing to remain on the peaks. Tarot imagery also affirms the high points of our meetings with our creativity, compassion and joy. These are some of the moments through which we refine our understanding of life's mysteries; of truth, life, death, love and power.

The exact origins of tarot cards remain concealed from

us and there is much debate about their genesis. References to tarot date back to the fourteenth century. It is commonly held that the Romany people brought tarot to Europe, perhaps from Egypt or India. However, it is not the intention of this book to focus on a historical analysis of tarot. It is significant that the framework of tarot has survived for six centuries. The perennial appeal of tarot assures us this is by no means a New Age fad.

Since 1985, when I began to use tarot, I have searched for a deck which eclectically expressed the breadth and profundity of the traditional tarot within a visual context relevant to current issues. I came to realise that the text and images I sought were actually close at hand — contained within me and arising from a multitude of experiences. These imaginings have been given their full beauty and meaning through the strength of Dwariko's intuitive artwork.

Songs for the Journey Home is a re-visioning of tarot, reflecting the issues we face as we rapidly approach the twenty-first century, although this deck also draws strength and sustenance from tarot's mythical roots. This deck retains the outward form of traditional tarot, with a total of seventy-eight images. The twenty-two cards known as the Major Arcana have been renamed the Life Songs. In the text the analogy of the four seasons is used to describe the powerful cycles of change which create the major contours of our experiences.

The sixteen cards known as the Court cards have been renamed the Shell Songs. Traditionally the Court cards depict pages, knights, queens and kings. Here, they are renamed Innocence, Awakening, Creating and Resolving. They represent the experiences we have through inhabiting the shell of the physical body and through the roles we take on. They also symbolise our freshness and maturing within individual situations.

The forty images traditonally known as the Minor Arcana are renamed the Hearth Songs. These images reflect the day-to-day learnings which we have from our immediate environment. We are often so close to these experiences that we may not be able to spot the repetitive patterns which disempower us. Incongruity between daily life and espoused spiritual values are also highlighted here.

These forty cards are traditionally divided into the four elemental themes of earth, fire, water and air and are typically named Pentacles, Wands (or Rods), Cups and Swords. These elemental qualities have been retained in this deck as follows: the Pentacles become Earth Songs; the Wands become Flame Songs; the Cups become Wave Songs; and the Swords become Wind Songs. Each of the four elemental groups has images numbered from one to ten. These numerical pathways follow through from the conception to the maturing of practical aspirations, inspirations, feelings and thoughts.

Songs for the Journey Home depicts the meditative journey and the need for spirituality and practical action to become unified. Action is most effective when it is grounded in the context of the spiritual journey; otherwise the longing to bring healing to the Earth will be a precarious whim, disrupted by personal power plays and sideline agendas.

In the past decade there has been a tremendous global awakening and recognition of the fact that we live on a planet in jeopardy. Now, not only small pressure groups but also governments are addressing environmental issues both nationally and internationally. In these times of environmental catastrophes these tarot images show us that we must go beyond the temples and be able to recognise the messages given to us by the hills, the water, the caverns and the trees. We must sensitively listen to the Earth.

Dwariko and I wish to acknowledge the struggles of indigenous peoples throughout the world, who are seeking to retain or reclaim and protect their cultures, heritages, religions and guardianship of the Earth Mother. However, we have not appropriated symbols of indigenous peoples as these are not ours to use by birthright or initiation. We have chosen, rather, to convey our love for Earth through simple elemental imagery.

In *Songs for the Journey Home* we, as the authors, have sought to provide a gender balance in the imagery and throughout the writing. However, every image may be seen, in one context or another, as a reflection of each person's strengths, frailties and efforts. Our own concerns regarding the repressive and controlling nature of patriarchal ideologies and systems are evident through the images and the text. *Songs for the Journey Home* does also vividly acknowledge the life-affirming commitment of many of the Earth's sons, who use the scientific mind in harmony with the heart to bring about healing and an end to domination.

In many of the images we have made a radical move away from traditional Western mystery symbology. This reflects the understanding, borne out through life experiences, that, although the great truths are profound, they are hidden in divine simplicity. For example, we are perhaps more likely to have a major realisation while putting our whole heart and soul into weeding the garden than we are while squirming in a state of heightened discomfort, trying to achieve some obscure meditation posture.

The way to significant personal insights is also through laughter. Therefore some images such as the Fool, the Chariot and the Hanged One do depict what may appear to be irreverent interpretations of the traditional archetypes. Laughter loosens the body and floods us with a sense of well-being. This makes it easier for us to recognise the choices which will bring us the most happiness.

There are many pathways from which to approach tarot. Essentially much of the fun and the magic of tarot begins when we use a selection of the cards, laying them out as a representation of our emotional, mental, creative, physical and spiritual realities. These images are commonly chosen intuitively, with all the cards face downwards. They are then often placed in a pattern, with the placement of each card having a particular emphasis. This pattern is known as a tarot layout. With a tarot reading, it is the interplay of the various images as much as the individual images themselves which is important. For example, a tarot layout will show us whether we have many different opinions about a decision we are contemplating or whether we are feeling totally fine about the choice we are making.

A difficulty some people grapple with is the question of how it is possible to make anything other than a random choice from the images when they are all placed face downwards. I have always felt that each card has a vibrational quality which we are drawn towards. This belief has been heightened through the process of creating *Songs for the Journey Home*. Each image represents hours of meditation, storytelling, dreaming, waiting, receiving, laughter, tears, friendship and love. I am sure that everything that has led to the birth of each card is energetically retained in the image. I also know that old tarot decks have a very powerful vibrational quality, as they are full of all the stories they have ever told.

However, if choosing the cards intuitively does not suit you, then look for images which attract your attention, whether or not you understand their meanings. A wonderful way to come to know the cards is to select one to meditate on each day.

I suggest you first read through the book, looking at the cards as you move through the various interpretations of the imagery. This will help you to develop a sense of the qualities of the Life Songs, the Shell Songs and the Hearth Songs. It is very useful to lay out the images in their groupings rather than thinking of tarot as seventy-eight totally unconnected cards. The Life Songs use the pattern of the seasons. The Shell Songs use the context of human development, from childhood to maturity, as well as elemental themes. The Hearth Songs use numerical and elemental patterns.

You may find working with the creative visualisations in the book helps you to make contact with your creative, intuitive inner world. The myths and stories which have been an integral part of creating *Songs for the Journey Home* will, I hope, encourage you to tell your own stories.

The portions of the book which focus on tarot layouts and how to go about tarot readings are guidelines and suggestions. Every person approaches readings differently and there are no rigid rules. Beware of people who say there are! The one rule I have for myself is that I must always focus on the energetic jewel at the centre of the person I am reading for. This means I approach the person with love in my heart and respect for their journey, no matter what disturbances I perceive ruffling the surface of their Being. If I am unable to behold the person in this way, through judgments I may have, then I must recognise my limitations and not enter into a relationship with this person through a tarot reading. This is not to reflect negatively on the other person, but rather to realise I am not the appropriate one to serve this person right now.

Learning to read tarot may be likened to entering a room full of people you do not know — there is an awkwardness. Yet, as you look around, you are immediately attracted to some people, intuitively recognising the possibility for connection. With others, there may be an active drawing away — perhaps a reflection elicits some discomfort in you. In the same way, with some tarot cards I have immediately dived deep; others have taken years to befriend and to feel a true sense of understanding the imagery.

Fortunately, my initial learning of the cards came about through many hours of sitting with my friend Lizi. She gave me the courage to read what I saw with my fresh eyes, to take time, to be patient, to allow silence and to let the images work within. From the very beginning, I have experienced the cards as each having a distinct and subtle essence, yet, at the same time, a very fluid interpretation, dependent on the interplay with all the other cards in the reading and the energy I perceive within the person I am reading for.

While this book offers contemplations on each card, avoid allowing rigid interpretations to enter your readings. No image can be assigned one fixed meaning. Through the magic of tarot — the true magic — an energy field builds up between the reader and the friend and is released through the reading. This particular layout will never occur again, nor be read in exactly the same way.

So enjoy your tarot journey as much as Dwariko and I continue to enjoy ours.

The title *Songs for the Journey Home* reflects the learning

Dwariko and I received during our time as devotees of Bhagwan Shree Rajneesh, the spiritual teacher we speak of in the two chapters which follow. From him we learned the importance of feeling the joy and the fragrance of the many moments which make up the journey of life. How important it is to feel our inner Being dance and sing with the earth and the sky and with all the experiences which flow towards us. How important it is not to miss the music of life, whether it is a lullaby, a serenade, a chant or a requiem.

Songs for the Journey Home visually portrays the experience of listening to an inner sound — perhaps a voice — which draws us ever closer to living more and more frequently in harmony with our own personal sense of 'being on the right track'. It is not a matter of moving forward in time toward that nebulous and elusive goal of enlightenment but, rather, dancing backwards: whirling and spinning back through and behind the veils of repression, conditioning, guilt and pain, until we feel our body, both as a physical and spiritual reality, experiencing new levels of freedom and, therefore, creativity and love.

To sing the song of our journey is to embrace the opportunities for gaining greater sensitivity, towards ourselves and others. Instead of creating hierarchies of experiences, labelling times of prayer and meditation as having greater value than other events we may label as mundane, we come to experience our life as an interwoven whole. Thus we feel an increasing sense of integration and consistency between our inner and outer life.

Eventually a song arises from the pool of silence at the very centre of our Being — this is our Homecoming Song.

Catherine's story

I have had a fascination with the metaphysical realms of human experience for the greater part of my life, with memories of a search for meaning reaching back to when I was about seven or eight years old. Initially, the only external learning and guidance available to me was through Christianity. As an adolescent I was particularly attracted to pentecostal churches, as I loved the passionate immersion in energies I little understood.

However, a marriage break-up ostracised me from the Church, as I became increasingly frustrated and intolerant of the prevailing Christian attitudes towards women. I also felt extremely confused. I wanted to express my spiritual nature, but felt my womanhood being squeezed into a 'good little woman' mode. I was also unable to reconcile the essence of Christ, which I believed I contacted in prayer, with the rigid and constraining biblical teachings.

I distinctly remember a conversation with the minister, just prior to my separation from my husband. I knew I had to leave my marriage as the relationship was crumbling. This first love had foundations of romantic love that were too fragile to support us. I longed for a depth of intimacy which also allowed space for each to flourish individually.

I asked this minister, 'What do I do if the Word of God, as written in the Bible, is different from what I feel inside that I must do?' He replied, 'You must trust the Word of God — it is the Truth.'

I knew then, painful though it was, that I was on my own spiritually. I continued to seek an understanding of the evolution of human consciousness. At the same time, I was often baffled by the misery so many affluent people were living in. My nursing career meant I was constantly confronted with life's mysteries, and so many times I felt the sacredness of death as the life-source leaves the body.

Intimate relationships became my teachers. Many friends could never make out a pattern in the partners I chose. I now recognise that I chose lovers who each reflected a distinctly different aspect of myself. These relationships all foundered — although they were passionate and dramatic! In them, I would live fully in only one aspect of myself. When I moved on to experience another part of myself — the polar opposite of the energy field I had been in — there would be a change in partners as well.

Books also became my teachers as I read with voracity. Authors who particularly come to mind from this period, during my early twenties, are Erich Fromm, Eric Berne, Carl Rogers and Arthur Janov. I now note that during this part of my life it was men's writing, rather than women's, which shaped my thinking.

In 1982 I was introduced to the writings of Bhagwan Shree Rajneesh and I became involved with a small group of his disciples in Auckland. I at last felt that I had found a spiritual teacher who did not deny the human experience and who, in particular, did not deny the power of women's intelligence, intuition, sensuality and ability to connect easily with a sense of the divine. The years from 1982 to 1985 were volatile, ecstatic, dramatic and despairing years, through which I tried to meditate. In reality, however, I was far more fascinated with the cathartic and intense experiences offered in the therapy groups run as an adjunct to meditation training.

By the time I became a disciple of Bhagwan's, he and his commune had moved from Poona, India, to Oregon, U.S.A. I travelled there three times. The love, magic and mystery I experienced on the commune's ranch released some of the most intense emotional experiences I had ever had. However, this emotional intensity clouded my inner vision, and there was much I chose not to see. The events which led to the cataclysmic end of this commune, Rajneeshpuram, had been in motion for a long time but so many of us only recognised the corruption and misuse of power in hindsight.

In 1983 I had moved to Sydney, Australia, and in 1985 I became a member of the Rajneesh commune there, only five months before the collapse of our Oregon headquarters. The internal scandals of our organisation made headlines in many parts of the world. I was devastated when I recognised how blind I had been. I left the disintegrating Sydney commune with Lizi and we moved into an apartment together. The months that followed were dark and questioning times. We both felt raw and wounded for many months.

Lizi, also a disciple of Bhagwan's, used tarot in a skilled and intuitive way — a fine blend of wisdom, practicality, therapeutic skills and a large dash of humour. This ability had, for the most part, been put aside during her time in the commune, but was drawn out again during our many evenings together. We were desperate to understand the spiritual abyss we had fallen into, yet we were reluctant to go outside ourselves again to seek the answers. The tarot images, reflecting profound archetypal crises and avenues for transformation, became mirrors of our process of reclaiming a sense of self direction and trust.

At first I was somewhat overwhelmed by the number of cards and the many pictures of people and symbols. I would sit with Lizi, listening and watching as she read for the numerous people who flowed in through our front door. Lizi would ask for my interpretations, which I would offer slowly and with extreme hesitation. I found that the cards initially released within me a kaleidoscope of images but I had difficulty in translating these pictures and my feelings about them into words. Lizi astutely gave me all the time I needed, gently teasing me about my 'mellifluous pauses'.

I continued my nursing work and attended a drama school for a year. The school used many psychodrama techniques and these, combined with the love and support of teachers and students, helped me to heal and gave me a breadth of perception as to why my spiritual world had collapsed.

During 1986 I returned to New Zealand for a holiday, reuniting with my parents with love and tears; they had been very fearful during my time as a sanyassin (devotee of Bhagwan) that I would be lost to them forever. I also met a friend from earlier years. This time there was instant attraction, and love has grown, creating in my life the most loving, satisfying and respectful relationship I have experienced with a man. At the end of 1986 I returned to live in New Zealand, with a strong sense of coming home. In the time away I had often felt a desperate longing to be with the familiar landscapes and sea.

I continued with my tarot readings, and sent taped recordings of layouts I would do for Lizi — thank God for the pause button on the tape deck! By looking at her photo and feeling my love for her a reading that was always apt for her situation would emerge. I began using the cards for meditation, using a different card each day and allowing my uncensored interpretations to flow. I found that writing my understandings bypassed the difficulties I experienced when trying to express the interrelated patterns I saw before me.

At times I felt a longing for some outward expression of the inner truth I felt — wanting to make my understanding real in the physical world. I knew that this expression would become stifled if I joined some organised group; I found myself to be very intolerant of the petty power plays which pervade many groups of seekers who journey together. My experience of despair when I left the Rajneesh commune left me with a very strong psychic radar for detecting the often subtly dogmatic, restrictive and controlling elements in groups with a therapeutic and spiritual intent.

I no longer had the outer trappings of a disciple. My mala was packed away, and gone were the rainbow-coloured clothes. I was known by my sannyas name, Bodhicharya, by only a handful of people. I began to glimpse the true ordinariness of the spiritual path — a degree of simplicity which, in the past, had seemed unattainable. Simplicity has come to mean having life full of dear and loving people, each journeying in their own ways. Simplicity is living at peace, where possible, and resolving conflict with minimal delay. It is the love and appreciation I have for the environment in which I live. It is good food, good wine, aesthetic surroundings and creative projects. It is living in the world and getting on with the vast number of practicalities to be dealt with and seeing these as part of, and not separate from, the spiritual life.

I found, in particular, that my dear friend Dwariko, who was also a disciple of Bhagwan's, shared this understanding of the simplicity of life. I would read the tarot for her, not to solve any great problems but as an instrument for eliciting self knowledge in each of us. We had known each other for years, our affinity drawing us together. She and Lizi also held a great fondness for each other, having worked closely together in the Sydney commune.

As I used the cards for a focus in meditation, I searched through all the tarot packs available in this country, seeking images which more clearly expressed the depth of meaning I sensed in each card. Simultaneously, through meditating in the cards, ideas would come about their meanings that were at variance with interpretations I had read elsewhere.

The yearning for a tarot deck which expressed my true understanding of the images came to a sudden turning point on 17 May 1989. Dwariko was driving Gitika and me to the airport. I was doing a mad reading for Gitika in the back seat of the car before she flew off on a selling trip to Australia. Somehow, in the midst of all the good humour, with cards falling everywhere and all of us in on the reading, discussing the relevance of Gitika's forthcoming trip, the idea of writing a book and creating a new deck came. I felt a tremendous surge of rightness which has remained with me throughout the project.

I poured out my ideas to Dwariko before flying off for a week's holiday in the South Island with a close friend. While Diana worked during the day, I sat in her delightful cottage, looking out to snow-covered mountains, and wrote the framework of the book and the structure the deck would take.

In November 1989 Dwariko gathered together the courage to draw the first card — she chose to do the Sun — an exquisite beginning. From this time on, the true mutuality of the project was in full swing. Many, many times we have sat together — writing and drawing in harmonious companionability — with an ebb and flow of chatting and silence, questioning and clarifying. I discovered I was able to put my visions for many of the cards into rough pencil sketches to convey to Dwariko the essence I sought.

Dwariko and I have worked together on the project with an extraordinary degree of harmony, good will, good humour and, at times, overflowing exuberance — particularly each time a new card was born and each time I found words to express the qualities of the images.

It's 20 October 1992. Dwariko has finished drawing and painting all the cards except the Homecoming, which she's been saving to last. I've nearly finished the writing and the tarot image which most strongly reflects my feelings right now is Renewal. Again this morning I woke in the early hours, as I have so often throughout the three-and-a-half years of the project. Sleep and dreaming have been powerful times of alchemy for me, a time when the mass of images and words which flood my wakeful consciousness shift and settle. Before I go to sleep each night I ask for the symbols which will best portray the experiences I am wanting to write about. I also ask for ways to most clearly interpret imagery so that the meanings of the cards will be lifted out of obscurity to become accessible and relevant tools for transformation. Sometimes the seeds of my requests are planted weeks or months before there is evidence of any growth of an idea, and this I have also come to trust totally.

This morning, lying in the dark, I vaguely recalled a dream I had some years ago, tantalisingly flickering in my memory. Getting up, I searched through a number of folders, as I knew I had recorded this dream somewhere. Eventually I found it. On 12 May 1989 I had dreamt I was on the Rajneeshee ranch in Oregon. I knew I had died. I went to a field which had a wooden fence around it. The field was newly ploughed. I was given an urn, which contained my ashes. I took the urn away and sprinkled my ashes. I was alive in this current body at the time, yet I also knew these were the ashes of this body.

This is all the detail of the dream I had written. I then looked up the date of the wild, flowing, mad day when the vision for the project came rushing in to me. It was five days after this dream. It seems to me this tarot work has been my phoenix rising, and the renewal of my trust in the unseen realms which exist beyond known forms.

Dwariko's Story

I had the rare opportunity in 1989 to put almost everything on hold for the year and to take the time to evaluate the direction and purpose of my life. I was living with my two daughters, renting a cottage in a central city suburb. This home was a real place of retreat, surrounded by huge native trees. The atmosphere of seclusion enhanced my efforts to achieve as little as possible. Whenever I had a choice whether to do, or not to do, I chose the latter.

On one of the rare occasions during this reflective year when I chose to do, rather than not to do, I drove my friends Bodhi and Gitika to the airport. I'll say here that Catherine was known as Bodhicharya when I met her and she'll always be Bodhi to me. Anyway, Bodhi was full of high spirits, and in the time it took to drive to the city's airport she'd decided to write a book on tarot.

In the gap between dropping Gitika off at the international airport and taking Bodhi to the domestic terminal, she'd decided that I was the person to transform the fleeting images she was constantly seeing into a tarot deck. This is seventy-eight pieces of artwork we're talking about. And my career as an artist was so 'on hold' it was virtually non-existent. But what can you do when your good friend asks a favour and smiles at you as if all she's wanting you to do is give up a small part of your spare time, which you obviously have a lot of, to help her out a little? Bodhi has a persuasive way with words and I found myself grinning back and saying yes. I mean, what chance was there I was going to be held to it?

It's just as well she didn't say, 'Dwa, how about drawing seventy-eight images which reflect, in one way or another, everything you've ever experienced? And by the way, while you do it, you'll remember so much that you thought you'd forgotten, and you'll have nightmares, night after night at times. And in the process you'll remember and relive the journey from when your creativity flowed through you as a child and began to flower fully in you as a young woman. You'll recall the drying up of your creative sap before a full ripening was reached, as far as your artwork was concerned.' And fortunately, because Bodhi doesn't see herself as a fortune-teller, she didn't gaze through the veils of time and tell me, 'For most of the time, while you're working on this project, you'll teach at high school full-time, continue to be the sole active parent in raising your girls, have a weekend catering job as you'll be short of cash and you'll also revive your flute playing to a standard whereby you'll have pupils. In your spare time, you'll do the artwork.'

The extraordinary experience of creating a tarot deck has evolved step by step. Bodhi kept giving me photocopies of her writings about the cards. We went to a series of tarot classes a friend was running as, at this time, Bodhi was so immersed in details she found it impossible to give me an overview. These classes with Anupasana were the taste I needed to give me the impetus to begin. I began with the Sun, jotting down key phrases from Bodhi's writing around the edges of my art paper, then closing my eyes and seeing the words transform into pictures. It took two attempts to arrive at a Sun I felt happy with, and I then moved on to the Star. Bodhi would drop in regularly, as I lived en route to the hospital where she worked. The 'birth' of each new image was utterly magical and a true reward after the struggles or disturbances which had arisen in me in the creative process.

After these first two images it seemed a huge task to conjure up another seventy-six pictures. It was then that Bodhi tentatively asked if I would like some ideas and sketches from her. This was the beginning of our realising that by working on images together, the creative floodgates were wide open. The only parameter to which we were both committed was that we would write about and create images from our own experiences or observations. In this way, we could be certain that, even if the project didn't have universal appeal, we could rest assured that everything we had attempted to communicate could be verified from our own experience.

It's now February 1993 and all the images are complete. I'm

beginning a new school term, doing what I love to do, teaching art. The title of the project, *Songs for the Journey Home*, fits perfectly with my experience of seeing the pathway which has led me to this moment. As I review my life's experiences thus far, I see that my ability to express myself through art is a treasure I was unable to recognise and appreciate fully when I was in my twenties. I almost lost sight of this gift for some years.

I reflect on how easily my artwork flowed as a child, sitting beside my mother as she painted and doing my own paintings. At school, this passion for art was largely discouraged. A careers advisor thought I would be best suited to becoming a filing clerk. Fortunately, a few teachers came to my rescue, recognising my ability and encouraging me. I always remember Don Binney for this support.

The major dilemma I had was this: I had a longing to fit in and be ordinary, but to allow my artwork to flow through me gave rise to extraordinary feelings and perceptions I didn't know 'normal' people had. This yearning to fit in arose because to be in any way different in the New Zealand school system during the 1950s and 1960s was painful. I was different without even trying. With the surname von Sommaruga I cringed from day one of the roll call. The only other kid who suffered along with me was a Subritzky. To add to this, my father was a German from Berlin, interned for part of the Second World War in Australia before serving in the Medical Corps in Ghana. He was Jewish at a time when the only two camps of religious worship deemed appropriate were Catholic and Protestant.

I did achieve my dream and go to art school. However, it didn't remain my top priority for long. I qualified with a degree in Fine Arts and went on to train as a teacher, which gave me an income as well as allowing me to be immersed in the subject I loved.

My mind flicks through the years now, years which included marriage to a man I ended up spending seventeen years of my life with. He is the father of my two children. I loved the early years of mothering and homemaking, before the relationship soured beyond resolution through my husband's violence. During my marriage most of my creative energies went into nurturing my children. Forays back into my world of art were met with open hostility from my husband, unless my efforts led to some financial gain. I made novelty bags, pillows and pottery jewellery boxes to sell. I also turned to renovating our home. These were useful and therefore acceptable ways of keeping my creativity alive.

I recall in 1979 entering a competition for an illustrated book for children under five. My husband was furious to see me so selfishly wasting time while he was out working, but in this instance I was not deterred. I would wake myself up while he and the children slept and in this way I completed the story-poem and drawings. My work was well received, although the prospective publishers wanted me to change so much of my work it would have become unrecognisable and, as I saw it, lose much of its charm. Nine years later I independently published it as a diary.

For the most part, however, it was more painful to have only a taste of my untapped potential than to shut down altogether. The taste was the reminder of what I'd left behind and didn't know how to reclaim. Eventually I realised I was living in my husband's world and had given up on my own world. With two young children, though, the fear of how I would cope if I left my husband held me back. And then a friend came to my rescue by running off with him! I can still feel the exhilaration which flooded through me the day he left. Any difficulties I have experienced as a mother bringing up children alone seem minuscule in comparison to the glorious freedom I have experienced since he left.

Once my husband left I was determined there would be no weakening of resolve on my part, should he wish to come back. With money from our settlement I spent a year with the girls, travelling through the U.S.A., Canada and Europe, regaining a sense of myself and realising I was absolutely capable of making decisions.

On my return to New Zealand an unexpected turning point came, one night when I went to a party. I met a man who had the strange name of Vilas. He had a mop of curly hair, wore red clothes and had beads around his neck. A locket with a photograph of a grey-bearded man's face hung from the beads. When I sat next to this Vilas, I was utterly shocked by the physical jolt of electricity which passed between us. Before this moment, I had never experienced such a feeling, thinking such notions were only found in the realms of romantic fiction. The love affair I began with Vilas expanded to a love affair of the heart with his spiritual teacher, Bhagwan Shree Rajneesh.

I began going to the local centre where this teacher's disciples gathered, regularly participating in the meditations and listening to videotaped discourses. My whole body reacted in ways which frightened me: I was finding it hard to walk and my body frequently shook uncontrollably. I realised I needed help and rang a therapist, Brian Knight. When he saw me, he reassured me there was nothing physically wrong with me. He explained that the body responds in this way when emotional constrictions are released from the body through meditation. I began to feel the embers of an energetic fire coming alive and blazing within me. Brian Knight asked me to illustrate his book, *My Feelings Are My Friends*, which was a wonderful opportunity to reconnect with my love of art.

I became a disciple of Bhagwan's and was given the name Dwariko. This was my awakening to the fullness of who I am. I also realised that I could do all I love to do without becoming in any way constricted by defining myself according to my activities. I notice people respond so differently, depending whether I meet them in my role as a teacher, a mother, an artist, a flautist. It is not that I mind people knowing my capabilities. It is the expectations other people try to foist upon me I object to.

This differentiation is very important to me: we do what we love to do, but we are not these outer roles. I never wanted to be defined as an artist but, rather, one who loves to draw; not the Mother, but the person who nurtures her children; not the teacher, but one who teaches. I am still the same person through all these shifting surfaces. It is not the role which brings me joy, it is the conscious choosing of where and how I will direct the energy of my life force. I want to be seen as just me, knowing this sense of me will also ultimately dissolve when I die.

When I look back I remember that, as a young woman doing my artwork, I only felt good while I was actually doing the work; when I wasn't, I felt miserable. I see this whole journey away from my artwork took me through experiences from which I learned I have to feel good in myself first. Now I do feel wonderful most of the time, whether I'm creating tarot cards, or teaching, or cooking, or anything. This is what being with Bhagwan and being with his sanyassins has taught me. The learning is now being carried further through the teachings of Barry Long, another spiritual teacher.

The split I once experienced, wanting to be ordinary and yet extraordinary, has now healed, even though people still struggle with my surname! In the past I associated being extraordinary with religious and racial identification and I associated ordinariness with the anonymity of mediocrity. Now I discover that the ordinary and the extraordinary have merged, because now extraordinary means coming alive and expressing my own unique qualities and being true to myself. Ordinary has also become just fine, too, because ordinary means not creating a split, so that everything is of equal value. These definitions have lost the loadedness they once had for me and I experience both simultaneously. The essence of the message I seek to convey throughout all the imagery is this understanding I have come to, of the blending together of the ordinary and the extraordinary.

The tarot image which currently expresses where I stand is the Tenth Earth Song. I now feel I have taken centre stage in the production of my own life. I pause and savour the joy of having completed the seventy-eight images. I know that as yet unenvisaged creativity awaits me. I reclaim my German origins in this image, which has the flavour of the magic of Berlin in the years before the Second World War. I know that I am able to fully express myself through collaboration, rather than being in competition with another person. This is portrayed by the relationship of the pianist and the singer — Bodhi and me. Our audience throughout the project has been a very small group of strong supporters, and the dearest faces are those of my beloved daughters, Sara and Emilie. To them I offer my love and encouragement, to keep listening for the themes and melodies of their own songs for their own journeys, as I now listen to mine.

AN OVERVIEW
of the Life Songs

The Life Songs, traditionally known as the Major Arcana (the Greater Secrets) are the theme songs of our life journeys. The Life Songs reflect experiences which resound powerfully within us. Although these experiences may be unsettling, they also lead us towards an ever greater degree of self knowledge and compassion. We come to see more clearly the inner forces which motivate our choices.

The twenty-two images which make up the Life Songs are presented here within the framework of the seasons. This seasonal context reminds us that the journey is not one of striving towards perfection, it is an ever-increasing sensitivity towards the cyclical nature of all things. If we try to impede the cycle of life, stagnation occurs. If we watch, we will notice similarities in the situations which keep entering the sphere of our personal experience. We are given many opportunities to respond with enquiry, rather than being purely reactive to events. We enter into an ever more unifying experience of recognising the ebbing and flowing, birthing and dying, waxing and waning nature of this life in the physical body.

Each season offers gifts, challenges and lessons. At the

centre of the Life Songs are the Fool and the Homecoming. These images are timeless and seasonless and their meanings are rarely easy to convey in words. They represent our yearning to reconnect with some deep inner quality for which we may have no name, the search for a depth of love, spontaneity, wisdom and self acceptance whereby we experience life as an integration of profundity and simplicity.

The progression of the Life Songs will now be followed in numerical order, with brief and therefore partial meanings of the images. You can find a full interpretation in the chapter devoted to each of the Life Songs.

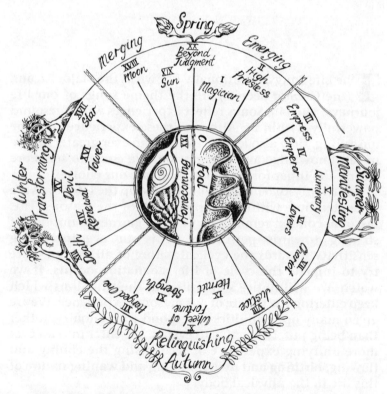

Seasons of the Life Songs

At the centre of the Life Songs The Fool (0) symbolises our instinctive nature and our ability to think laterally and creatively. The Fool takes great leaps of faith and lands on his feet.

Spring — Emerging The Magician (I) has experienced finding the key to the Kingdom of Heaven on Earth. He realises the contribution he is able to make through having had this experience. He has the intuition of the Fool and he combines this with action.

The High Priestess (II) uses all of her senses to discern the truth of a situation. Although she has highly developed powers of perception, she often remains silent as she has no interest in cajoling or attempting to convince another. She knows each person must seek their own truth through their own experiences.

Summer — Manifesting The Empress (III) is the sacred vessel through which new life comes. She represents the actual procreative power of women. She also signifies our willingness to lovingly and patiently nurture our creativity to fruition.

The Emperor (IV) indicates the desire for traditional boundaries and for a sense of security acquired through slotting into commonly accepted hierarchies. This security often requires compliance to the norms established by the group that wields the power. To rectify this imbalance the commitment and strength of a group rather than an individual struggle is often what is required.

The Luminary (V) gives us the vision of our experiences as a tapestry, woven with rich colour, each time we seek to express our true nature. The Luminary also asks us to examine the teachings we have received thus far. We are able to consciously choose to continue with learnings which lead us to a greater experience of wholeness. We release ourselves from teachings which stifle and control us.

The Lovers (VI) signifies relationships which take us to greater depths than we have been able to reach alone. The beloved mirrors to us the jewel which is at the centre of each of us. We also see reflected all the murky misery which holds us back from radiating our beauty.

The Chariot (VII) offers the challenge of staying committed to the path we have chosen, through the rough and the smooth. We need to be sensitive to the real call to change course as opposed to the fickle indecisiveness which keeps distracting us from our sense of purpose.

Autumn — Relinquishing   Justice (VIII) calls upon each of us to find some way to rectify an imbalanced and unjust situation. There is the possiblity for political and spiritual apathy here, or else we can choose to utilise this painful knowledge and take decisive action.

We become reflective, as seen in the Hermit (IX), seeking a depth of personal understanding in order to live in the world with a sense of purpose and harmony.

The Wheel of Fortune (X) reminds us we have the choice whether to keep reacting to the endless drama of life, or to witness the parade of events from a still and contemplative centre.

Strength (XI) represents the power of love, which is able to overcome seemingly insurmountable difficulties. This image also signifies being comfortable in the presence of our passion.

The Hanged One (XII) is the letting go of control. Through this experience we attain new perspectives which may supersede previous judgments and choices.

Winter — Transforming   Death (XIII) is a time of irrevocable change. We experience the sense of loss as we move from the familiar and on to the unknown. We are also aware of the new growth which will come through this transition.

Renewal (XIV) is the conscious recognition of the powerful process of transformation. The process is accompanied by an intensity and outpouring of feelings. This release brings to light old griefs and hurts which have previously lingered in the shadows. Now they are accessible for healing.

The Devil (XV) symbolises the pain and shame we carry, locked away in our memories. The Devil reminds us that until we make peace with our frailties we will constantly have the nagging feeling of being at war with ourselves. The card also signifies polarising judgments of good and bad, and right and wrong. This image sometimes represents the need for us to take up the role of devil's advocate, challenging the status quo.

The Tower (XVI) shows us how we remove ourselves from our joy, love and creativity, through becoming locked into rigid forms. There is no gracious way to exit. However, our departure gives us the opportunity to recognise how we became trapped in the first place. If we can see this clearly it will prevent a re-enactment of the same drama in a different set of circumstances.

The Star (XVII) is the healing of the inner rift and the experience of divine guidance and protection. This is the image of the healer. Through having faced our own dark night of the soul, we are able to reach out to others to offer loving encouragement.

Spring — Emerging The Moon (XVIII) is the willingness to follow step by step, along a path which is revealed a little at a time. It is only through walking the path that the way is shown to us. There may be maps which give the layout of the territory, but preparation of the logical mind will be but a small part of the process of discovery we are about to enter.

The Sun (XIX) signifies the inner work made visible, through a maturity of love, and a certain constancy of feeling at peace with ourselves. We achieve a comfortable balance of giving and receiving, and of relating and aloneness. We feel uplifted and our hearts are warmed by small occurrences and we enjoy the seemingly very ordinary events of our day-to-day existence.

Beyond Judgment (XX) signifies the wisdom which comes through allowing all of life to be our teacher and guide. Painful and difficult past experiences have drawn out qualities of strength, courage and compassion. We are able to detect pitfalls and to sidestep them. Our optimistic attitude is not dimmed by a cynical outlook.

At the centre of the Life Songs The Homecoming (XXI) is the wave of the spirit which enters the sacred vessel of the physical body. When we choose to become aware of this wave, we align ourselves to its cadences. A vibration like a song arises within us, calling us back into a deeper and deeper feeling of at-homeness within the body, and an at-oneness with all we perceive to be outside of ourselves.

THE LIFE SONGS
Tuning in to the Seasons of the Life Songs

The following exercise will help you become familiar with the emerging, manifesting, relinquishing and transforming qualities of the Life Songs. You may find it easiest to do this exercise before moving on to the in-depth interpretations of the twenty-two Life Songs.

Lay out the cards of the Life Songs (see page 28) and read through the overview of the Life Songs, looking at each image in turn. Be aware of the seasonal flow of the imagery. Feel which phase you identify with most at this time in your life:

Spring — the end of an old way of being leads to new growth which must then be nurtured towards maturity.

Summer — the bud of creativity is nurtured to fruition. Then begins the process of releasing attachments in order for whatever has been brought to life to now be shared.

Autumn — letting go of habitual ideas about success and achievement allows the discovery of new ways of relating. A period of doubting and questioning is vital.

Winter — evaluating and reflecting may lead to changes which are accompanied by some sense of separating from or drawing to a close a particular phase of your life.

Be aware of the Fool and the Homecoming at the centre of the Life Songs. Throughout every season, the Fool offers spontaneity and fresh ways of seeing. The Homecoming reminds you to listen to your inner guide in order for you to fully appreciate the significance of the transitions you are making.

There may be several phases occurring simultaneously. For example, you may have a new career opening which offers you greater self determination and responsibility. This will require you to relinquish a previous role in which you may have felt very safe. At the same time you are thoroughly enjoying anticipating the emergence and manifestation of your abilities.

Choose a season to explore more fully. Find photographs and do some drawings that express the feelings evoked by it. Play music which heightens your ability to tune into this phase. Place symbols from your life beside the cards you most identify with. You may find a particular season brings to mind a powerful phase you have now passed through. Write down these experiences and the images that elicit these memories.

This exercise can be a very powerful sharing experience when entered into as a ritual with friends. Set aside several hours to learn from each other's experiences. The more associations and stories you have with each image the more the cards seem to become infused with the essence of each remembering they reveal.

The Fool

Here we encounter the Fool. Undeterred by the chasm separating two banks, the Fool has climbed up a sapling and, using its flexibility, reaches the other side with ease.

The Fool does not split possible and impossible; close and distant; can have and can't have. Neither is it a matter of the Fool choosing greener pastures. It is the Fool's eternal inquisitiveness and optimism which inspire these leaps of faith into the unknown.

The Fool often plays alone, shying away from people who seek to restrain this exuberance, as they issue dire warnings of possible perils. These misguided counsellors are unaware of the highly attuned survival instincts of the Fool. They are also oblivious to their own lost attunement with life. The Fool's experiences are incomprehensible to those who journey through life choosing safe and well-used routes, rationally and logically worked out years in advance.

Most plod along the path, eyes downcast, and do not see our friend, the Fool, sailing past. They are deaf to his shrieks of delight, as their heads are full of calculating how many more miles there are to travel. But some lift their eyes and inhale the Fool's joy. Witnessing true spontaneity and delight strikes a long forgotten chord, giving them the courage to make their own leaps into the unknown.

The Fool also represents the innocence of the child. To fully experience the trust, spontaneity and freshness of the Fool as a present reality, you may need to heal and make peace with events from your childhood.

You may be wondering why the Fool is clothed, not a naked free spirit. The clothing symbolises children's right to have their own inner world — their own privacy. Children are so often perceived as possessions and are paraded as commodities, expressing parental aspirations.

From a very young age, children yearn for the space in which to create their own world, their own visions. This must not be intruded upon by adults. The child's rights to secrecy and dignity are so often violated by parents and other trusted relatives. When children are disrupted at a young age from privacy and a sense of having their inner world they then come out of their Being in order to survive. They begin to perform to outer expectations. This is the tragedy: the disconnection from wholeness forces the child to seek endless sources of gratification, as self love dims.

So many children are dragged to the outer circle of the Wheel of Fortune by parents who entrap the children in the parents' own dramas and calamities. We see this vividly portrayed in child-custody suits which make headline news. No wonder, as adults, the return to meditation seems an extremely difficult path to find — it was trampled on before it even emerged.

The Fool is instinctive and impulsive. If we are not in touch with our own inner Fool the response to seeing another's Fool may be disturbing. We may find ourselves feeling tremendous sadness as we look around at our neat and orderly lives, full of neat and orderly friends, and realise how stifled we feel. We may find the Fool too confronting and feel angry and irritated, wanting to squash and mould the Fool. If we use this opportunity to turn inwards we may open a door that has been firmly shut for too long. Let the Fool out and life will never be quite the same!

The Fool lives in each of us. Some keep their Fool locked in a box, only letting the Fool out when they are drunk. Some keep their Fool behind a curtained window — when they relax, we see the Fool peep out. Why do people keep their Fool so squashed? Is there no room in life for the unexpected?

The Fool is most often taken out and aired when we are sure no one else is around. Singing in the shower, we become the world-renowned opera star; speaking to the masses from the end of a vacuum-cleaner, we release the wild and witty orator within.

Leap out at people from behind the facades of whatever labels you have. Take a risk today. It doesn't have to be awesome or life-threatening — we can live our whole lives on the edge of the cliff and never actually fall off. In fact, we are far more tuned in as to just how far we can go.

Love lets the Fool run free, and those who are afraid of the Fool will avoid love. Yes, they may be suave and sexually competent in a gymnastic way, but they will veer away from love. The Fool loves to love and be loved — a wild madness arises which loses all cool and calm.

The Fool is the reclaiming of the inner child, responding to the circus of life with a fine blend of naivety, insight, humour and inquisitiveness.

The Magician

Imbibe the image of the Magician. He has in his heart a passionate desire for wholeness. The Magician loves the Earth. Gently, he cradles her in his left arm. With his right hand his energy is focused on action. The needle is a symbol of active intelligence, piercing to the very core of disharmony and corruption. The Magician is not content merely to reveal the source of discord. The thread is the continued commitment to taking action which will bring conciliation and reparation to the Earth.

A fresh breeze blows through this enchanted garden, indicating openness to new ideas and attitudes. The light of the rising sun merges with the Magician's aura. This yellow glow confirms his creative wisdom and desire for justice.

We see the intertwining of two vines. The red flowers reveal to us the Magician's passionate love for life. They intermingle with the white flowers, which reveal the Magician's purity of intent. Each moment is lived with utter fullness and respect. The walls upon which the vines grow are made from the clay of the Earth — she is the source of protection when we work to serve her. The gates of this sanctuary are closed. We are each to seek and find within ourselves the key to the Kingdom of Heaven on Earth. For Heaven is not another place: Heaven is a way of perceiving the present moment.

The Magician is no Atlas, labouring under the weight of the heavens and burdened by the enormity of the task. He kneels upon the Earth and draws his strength from her. The tilled soil beneath him looks almost like wings. Intensity and lightness — this is the Magician.

The Magician understands the Fool. The Magician sees the pattern, grasps the core and tastes the essence, then utilises this knowledge to direct his creativity. The Magician is able to blend life's elements so that their sum is greater than their separate parts.

He is strong with the desire to make a difference. This passion is fired from above and below: an intelligent and well-developed mind, combined with a continuing sense of service to the Earth who has given life and breath to the Magician.

The Magician has global vision and is intelligent enough to recognise the specific service he is able to give. The Fool dreams many dreams but it is the Magician who has the gift of insight as to which dream to follow. Here is the harnessing of inspiration, and trust that commitment to the vision will bring outcomes even bolder than the dream.

The Magician is subtle, recognising that there are many ways in which dreams can become manifest. The Magician often works surrounded by onlookers who do not recognise what is happening before their eyes. Many Magicians work in the world, bringing about extraordinary change which is recognised by people who work alongside them only in hindsight.

At times the Magician will draw away from much of the world, because a sense of safety and sanctuary may be required to further the vision. Where a vision is in the preparatory stage, it is vulnerable to being crushed by harsh logic and linear thought. At this time the treasured hopes are shared only with people who know the magic of transformation and have seen this process in their own lives.

Some may apprentice themselves to the Magician, although the Magician may not actively teach. The learning is by osmosis. The apprentice will never drain the Magician, because the Magician is nourished by the earth and the sky, the wind and the stars. The Magician does not seize this sustenance rapaciously. This food for the spirit flows in through love, prayer and gratitude, then flows out and beyond — ripples of healing, courage and service to life.

The Magician takes the stuff of everyday life and changes it before your eyes. The inner fire brings all polarities to melting point, and this very flame purifies the ego. To be a Magician means a willingness, not a destination.

The High Priestess

'I am the eternal birthplace and source of feminine mysteries, which are not lightly divulged and remain unseen by casual perusers.

'I am the essence of the poetry named Woman. I am the fragrance of all the flowers and the fields. And like the salt winds from the oceans, my truths will bring tears to your eyes.

'I am the well-spring of Woman's creativity, conscious love, intelligence and wisdom.

'I am sheltered within a cavern — one of the manifold wombs of the great Mother. I am the seed of feminine knowing, sheathed in a golden husk, which opens to reveal the everlasting flame burning at the centre of the Earth and within the belly, heart and mind of every woman.

'This knowledge of truth comes to me through inner sensations and images, rather than through logic, so I am slow to speak and use no other reference points than my own understanding and experiences.

'For all women, everywhere, if they choose to seek me within, I am the provider of unceasing strength and nourishment. See, my hair becomes the roots of the Empress Tree, conduits which will channel from the source to individual acts of creativity.

'I am loathed, mistrusted and, above all, feared by the Patriarch.

'Endless attempts are made to seduce the Empress into drawing sustenance from sources other than me and to fall in supplication before male gods.

'I am deep within each woman, if she should choose to listen.

'Some men will discover me — those who journey deeply through love and meditation will find themselves before me. I will recognise their quest and bless them.

'I will illuminate, ignite and then melt all pain, trauma and self deception, refining you so that you, too, become a true child of the Earth.'

To meet with the High Priestess, we must enter into her Cave of Silence, where she waits with eternal patience. She will not call us. We must recognise our own yearning to go to her. It is very easy to lose touch with the High Priestess, because so much of the Western World reinforces women's external presentation, with absolutely no recognition of the timeless inner sanctuary within Woman.

The essence of the High Priestess is paradoxical, because she is both phenomenally powerful and exquisitely sensitive and fragile. We see her incredible vitality when we are willing to respond to the inner voice calling us to her. Then we will see our whole lives shift and change as a result of this listening. However, this tremendous energetic source may be ignored for long periods, as we need to pause long enough and remain still enough to hear her voice.

The High Priestess is the sap and life blood of Woman. When Woman becomes separated from her true nature all manner of addictions and emotional dramas arise in an unconscious attempt to inadequately recreate the connection with the Source.

Self love returns us to self listening, although self love is portrayed as selfish and dangerous by those who prefer that Woman remains separated. The High Priestess is the expression of inner unity: she will reveal to us all incongruities which create within us experiences of being cut off from parts of ourselves.

Her words may seem harsh, but only because they are stripped of all cushioning. Cruelty is not her intention, but truth, for those who are fast asleep, is like a searing heat.

If we are willing to meet with the High Priestess we tap into a phenomenal source of compassionate power and wisdom. We recognise ourselves as both sacred and sexual beings. This takes some getting used to because the experience is the antithesis of the docile images of feminine spiritual expression which have been fed to women for centuries by male-dominated religions. Ultimately a full reclaiming of Woman Spirit occurs.

The Empress

The Empress awakens within us our yearning to live a life imbued with creative expression, with tremendous harmony existing between body and spirit.

Woman is portrayed here as the Empress Tree, pregnant with new life. She symbolises actual procreative power and the desire to provide nurturance and sustenance for another human being. She also signifies a potent psychic bond we may have with a creative process in which we are currently engaged. Her womb represents our innate ability to create an environment in which the seed of our fertile imaginings may flourish.

The image of the growing child reminds us there may be a significant distance in time between the conception and actual birth of our vision. Impatience will only hinder our ability to sense the subtle processes occurring within us.

The protective arms of the Empress enfold her child. This is the mystery of the creative act — we awaken to a sense of awe, love and belief in the processes of metamorphosis and transformation. The unborn child is sheltered within the Empress Tree in a symbiotic relationship which will gradually unfold as an initiatory journey for both. This is one of the challenges the Empress gives us: to create, and to lovingly release our creations in due time, allowing them to take on their own life force.

Just as the actual child within the womb is tremendously affected by the physical, mental, emotional and spiritual state of the mother, so it is with all creativity. Unlike the actual child, our dreams, if left untended, may lie dormant and unrecognised within us for lifetimes.

The aura of blue around the Empress's head reminds us that she is not in a state of emotional reactivity. She has, with conscious awareness, become a channel for the expression of creativity, with all the diversity and breadth of commitment this entails.

The roots of the Empress Tree reach deep into the earth, beyond the reach of the fluctuating climate. We must have a sense of continuously nourishing ourselves, as we give to our dreams and allow them to become living realities. Her softly fronded branches move gently in the dawn breeze, indicating to us that deeply rooted choices need not give rise to rigidity. Here is a willingness to move with new ideas. The Empress blends ancient and sturdy wisdom with new growth.

The Empress Tree is an image of vulnerability as well as strength. Although able to withstand storms and droughts, she will wither in a perpetually hostile environment.

If the Empress loses contact with the High Priestess, she will forget her affinity with the Great Mother and become a pruned and grafted hybrid, bearing shapely but tasteless fruit. In striving to become someone other than herself, the truly glorious flowering which might have been is lost.

The waxing moon reminds us to become aware of the images, songs and phrases which fleetingly drift before us in those moments between waking and sleeping. The dawn light brings many shadows, and we must walk with trust along the path we sense beneath our feet. The glimmering light of the rising sun alerts us that soon our efforts will be rewarded and our visions will become tangible.

The sea behind the Empress is the Ocean of Bliss, the vast reservoir of abundant well-being and love where all separate rivers merge. Listen: the songs of the Great Mother are carried unceasingly, borne on the crests of the waves, to all those who are willing to hear.

The Empress alerts you to the necessity to tap into your creativity. For many people, this is not an easy matter, since creativity is often not nurtured, fed, watered and encouraged. The environment is most often set for the production of logical practitioners of life, although the expression of creativity is often envied from afar.

What do you want to create? The answer may be very clear to you. Think carefully; ask yourself for the images before going to sleep. Make sure you are responding to an inner desire. Break through the layers of conditioned responsiveness. Honour your creativity, for the accolade may only come from you. Let this be enough. Conformity will not fuel your creative fire.

Give birth to the lover, the artist, the musician, the gourmet cook, the dancer, the mother, the conservationist. Passionately nurture your dream. Hold it close, until you feel it in and around you, growing. Courage and patience will be necessary in order to see the fruit of your longing.

Allow your creativity to be an outpouring of your harmony and wellness. There is no need to thrash the body like a poor beast of burden — the treasure is within. It will still be there after a walk, after sleep, a meal, a chat with a good friend.

When this card relates to the actual desire to give birth to a child, allow this choice to be fully conscious. Ensure that, as the woman you are now, you are loved and cherished by those around you. This is the time to experience the mystery of Woman — Life-Giver. Allow all aspects of the Empress within you to live. Life must be imbued with creative expression, otherwise the creative act of conception and birth will lead to dissatisfaction.

The Empress represents the Earth Mother, who must be honoured, loved and worshipped. The Empress tells us we are answerable to Existence for our actions. She may call us to protect and nurture those who do not have power to save themselves — all her precious creations are under threat.

The Empress is a potent spiritual image, fully grounded in the physical reality, with total recognition of all the joy and all the pain this reality brings.

The Emperor

Meeting with the Emperor entails facing the ways in which we use power and the beliefs we have about power. The model of power which the majority of the world has utilised for centuries is the patriarchal model, one linked with conquering and destroying. Most of us have, to a greater or lesser degree, been imprinted from birth with the values of this model. To move beyond the model of domination and submission, we must first recognise the values which have infiltrated our belief systems to the extent that atrocities are the norm, and ever more violent acts are perpetrated at an international level, supposedly to keep us safe.

The image of the Emperor portrays both the patriarchal model and the partnership model. It is vital to recognise that partnership does not mean collapsing in a heap of cosmic oneness, denying obvious differences. It is, rather, the willingness to accept differences and, at the same time, find ways of cooperating for the benefit of all. The partnership model removes divisive beliefs of cultural, religious and gender superiority.

Traditional tarot decks commonly depict an Emperor who is a stern yet benevolent ruler, which may lull us into a false sense of security about the supposedly altruistic motives of the people who hold economic, political and military power.

When the experience of meeting with, or embodying attributes of, the Emperor occurs at a personal level, we have the opportunity to either collude with the status quo or respond from a fresh perspective. Choosing to collude often comes from the desire for the comfort of traditionally sanctioned boundaries and a sense of security through slotting into accepted hierarchies. However, this compliance generally requires acquiescence to the norms established by the group who wield control, economically and politically.

The Emperor claims authority over other people's destinies

and firmly believes he knows which decisions will serve them best. He will believe his ideas reflect the thinking of all right-minded people. Portrayed here as an implacable cliff-face, the Emperor sets himself apart from the everyday survival issues faced by the majority of the world's people.

The Emperor is from the earth, but he has become rigid and aloof. The fields close to the Emperor are barren and dying, here symbolising the effects of economic rapaciousness. In global terms, the Emperor represents Western hierarchical domination, the imbalance in the distribution of wealth, and the corporate tentacles that reach around the entire world — and squeeze.

Very few people are capable of ruling rightly. It is rare — extremely rare — for people who are given power in a hierarchical system to use it in a way which serves the highest good of all. To be an Emperor is to believe one has automatic rights and automatic wisdom; to have the acclaim of the people is extremely seductive. Many have sought and achieved positions of power in the world with the intention of bringing about humanitarian changes. However, even the best-intentioned leader must consciously continue on an inner journey. Too much listening to the roar of the crowd will dim the inner light and then arises a subtle falseness which becomes more and more obvious the further one moves away from the Centre of Being. Power needs to change hands — to be in the hands of many, to be on the move — to keep fresh and alive, without attachment.

The power of the Emperor is the power of the left brain and the power of achievement in the marketplace. The Emperor may well live and work in a tower, aloof from the shadow of oppression cast in the name of economic advancement. The Emperor must become the Hermit before any redress in the balance of power is possible. The first step is to recognise the assumptions about the use of power defined by the patriarchal model. The Hermit represents the courage to be alone, with no mirror to reflect the glory the Emperor attains from external sources. In utter aloneness the experience of power over another fades and in its place arises a sense of elemental vibrancy, free from the desire to dominate and subdue.

The tree-hands represent the willingness to cooperate and to work with the needs of the people, without leaving behind a trail of ecological despair. As human beings we do have an inner power source which is given expression through the passionate direction of our will, without being destructive. When this outward projecting energy is channelled by a group who are focused on positive change through partnership, a powerful experience of being on a collective vision quest unfolds.

The Luminary

The essence of the Luminary is the seeking of wisdom and a sense of meaning. The Luminary replaces the traditional Hierophant. At times we may be aware of actively initiating the search for a greater degree of knowledge and understanding. At other times, life seems to mysteriously present us with a series of situations — one unfolding after the other — and we sense we are receiving divine guidance, as each step is subtly yet clearly before us.

The Luminary often represents the experience of reflecting upon spiritual, religious or philosophical teaching we have received at some stage in our lives. We may be choosing the aspects of this knowledge we intend to carry with us, and recognising messages which no longer serve us. The Luminary may also signal a time when we share the learnings from our experiences with other people.

Depicted in the image is the Fool, setting out on his journey, and receiving some directions from an older journeymaker. The natural contours of an exquisite landscape unfold before them. This terrain represents the inner peaks, troughs and middle-ground which are inevitable along the way.

The Guide and the Fool stand together on a small mound. This hillock represents the conscious recognition of the journey's beginning point. However, much has already occurred unconsciously in the Fool's life, to prepare for this moment of recognition and saying to life, 'I am ready — show me the way.'

The Fool gazes towards a mountain in the distance which looks deceptively close. When we begin on a journey, we often think we see the peak to which we aspire. It is only upon reaching this pinnacle that we are able to see all which lies beyond. This is the nature of growth, creativity and spiritual knowledge: more is revealed when we arrive at the right place for more to be shown to us.

The valley below looks so tranquil, spreading out before the travellers. Yet the golden beach may be the quicksand of emotional reactivity, dragging us down with such intensity that we are distracted from our true destination. The harbour symbolises a future departure point, where we will need to leave behind the safe and the known, in order to explore further.

The islands on the horizon, illuminated by the rising sun, have a violet hue. These islands are aspects of our higher selves which we are not yet consciously acquainted with. In fact, we often only arrive at these distant shores when circumstances shipwreck us on these far beaches, forcing us to take a closer look at talents and possibilities which we have ignored for too long.

The scrubby bushes, the New Zealand manuka, hug the base of the mountain. This hardy plant is one of the first to regenerate following the devastation of the native forest; here they are symbols of renewal. Even when there has been great trauma and all which is natural, true and good seems to have been ripped away, the healing can come. Watch for it so you do not trample on the new growth.

The Sun symbolises the unveiling of the fullness of our Being. It is only partially revealed in this image, representing the importance of finding our own pace and rhythm in our journeymaking. Going crazy is one of the ways the psyche copes with being opened to too much information too quickly from the unconscious. Time for assimilation is vital in the process of personal transformation.

The Lovers

Through love we dive deep with the beloved. Two separate rivers of life, we join together, longing to meet and merge in total union.

The blue waters through which these bodies slide symbolise the purity found in love — we feel renewed, refreshed, restored, light and abundant. The flaming lotus towards which the Lovers glide signifies the glorious sensuality and joy to be found in love-making. The richly green centre of this flowering is the offering we make to each other: to give of the essence and fragrance of our love, unreservedly, not withholding our cherishing, willing to replenish the fire of love again and again.

To the right of these lovers is a mirror. As we become more aware of why we make the choices we do, we are increasingly likely to attract people with whom we feel a great affinity, and our relationships are accompanied by less and less pain. We come to recognise the true gift of love we receive through being in a relationship as we see, mirrored in the beloved, the depth of our own capacity to love.

When we love unconsciously, full of expectations, conditioning and demands, we believe the beloved is the source of all the joy we feel. Hence, we cling: 'I love you, I need you, I want you forever.' The beloved has only evoked the loving which is innately within us. We are beautiful, glorious beings, and love has revealed our authentic nature to us.

With day-to-day pressures and commitments it is easy to lose sight of each other, falling back on habitual responses and stereotypical expectations. If this goes on too long, we will eventually see the strangers we have become. We need to take time to enjoy each other, continually reacquainting ourselves with the fullness which attracted us together in the first place.

Enter the stream of life fully with the beloved. Be true to love, and love will remain alive and continue to grow within you throughout your whole life. You will not necessarily remain with the same lover. It is the essence of love which is retained, not as a memory but as a vibrant pulsation within you. Succumbing to maudlin sentimentality over lost loves will render you incapable of tapping into this well-spring within you and unable to recognise love in a different physical form.

To the left of the Lovers is the paradise we enter when we totally surrender to love. The lilies within this image remind us of the death which occurs amidst the exquisite flowering. This death is the release from all the attitudes and definitions imposed upon us by our culture and upbringing about what sort of relationship is most suitable for us. By examining and overcoming prejudices and boundaries we create a sacred garden in which love will proliferate.

When choosing a partner we often bring to light through our choice relationship patterns we have observed and absorbed since our childhoods. We may find we are mimicking these patterns, recreating tensions and dramas. At times we may feel like a ventriloquist's puppet, mouthing voices from the past. Often, conscious effort and painful observation are needed to break the cycle of repeatedly bringing to life old emotional scripts.

Many of us, through years of observing and being in the presence of limited love, have only a hazy idea of what we are truly seeking when we yearn for a love relationship. Initially, we may have many abrasive relationships with highly incompatible people. If we are unconscious about our motives and desires we create friction — we rub each other up the wrong way. But there is also the possibility that the pain of this friction will bring an alertness and start to wake us up. If we can escape feeling like a victim, and instead ask, 'Why am I hurting myself? Why do I keep creating chaos?' the learning will happen, faster and faster.

These relationships show us the harsh and unresolved polarities within ourselves. As we see this more clearly, awareness dissolves these polarities internally and we do not seek to act them out in the external world through choosing incompatible lovers. If the drama is overcome, the beloved becomes a clearer mirror, in which we look deeper, until we see not the other, but our own forgotten face of pure love.

Even if we begin with love that is relatively untainted, society has so many mechanisms that will contaminate this beauty unless the people involved have a commitment to remain as conscious as possible, each moment. The ritual of traditional marriage may be such a mechanism. In so many marriages the beauty of the ritual of union is lost in proprietary attitudes. It seems that when marriage occurs, the unconscious conditioning laid down in many of us since birth often bursts open to reveal all the ghosts of imposed attitudes and ideas. The difficulty is that these ghosts are not just from this lifetime. Ghosts from generations ago speak of how the marriage should be and the pressure to conform means the subtle breath of love is stifled.

Problems also arise when marriage is automatically placed in hierarchy above all other relationships. However, we become impoverished when we limit ourselves by placing this bond of union above friendships, love of kin, love of life and love of the Earth.

The essence of the Lovers card is not marriage as such. Rather, it symbolises the sharing with another a rich blend of freedom and commitment, intimacy and individuality. However, there continues to be in society the urge to reduce the intrinsic magic of love, passion and union to something others can understand and manipulate. Marriage does not necessarily mean the loss of the essence of love which brought two people together. It may be, however, that preordained structures may hinder, rather than enhance, the flourishing of a relationship.

In terms of tarot, the journey to mature loving begins by diving deep with the beloved, as portrayed in the Lovers card. Eventually, there comes the journey of aloneness, as seen in the Hermit. Once we are able to be truly alone, without misery, we rekindle our inner flame and emerge as the Sun, radiating love and warmth whether the beloved is with us or not.

The Chariot

Here we see the charioteer, getting his life together in the material, physical world, dealing with all the demands and choices presented to him. This image assures us it is entirely appropriate to have goals and to aim for these with a sense of purpose.

Do you recognise this landscape, seen first in the Fool card? The sapling has become a stronger, sturdier tree. It no longer retains the same flexibility, but it provides shade for rest and a home for a multitude of creatures. Do not fear change and maturity — everything has a natural evolution and beauty.

A bridge has been built across the chasm, reminding us not to reject relating to the world in a practical manner. Our minds are exquisitely designed for this purpose — filling out forms, booking airline tickets, driving according to road rules, paying the rent, learning a foreign language, repairing a bicycle. Not everything lends itself to great flights of fancy.

The charioteer takes the reins, acknowledging the persistence, sensitivity and focus required to bring a dream into physical reality. To see the path ahead is not enough. We have to keep sight of what is happening within our vehicle — the physical body. The image of the chariot and the creatures pulling it is a visual representation of the diverse elements within, of which the charioteer needs to remain aware. Otherwise he will find himself continually distracted, up dead ends, and in hostile terrain perhaps suited to other people but not right for him.

The Chariot sailing above the Earth signifies our learning to journey lightly, without leaving chaos behind us. For too long, too many have 'left their mark' during their years within the physical body, leaving a scarred and shattered planet.

The Chariot itself has the appearance of loose armour around the charioteer, although it does not encase or restrict him. It is perfectly intelligent to take care out in the world, which seethes with reactivity and pain. Learn to look after yourself in practical ways: take self-defence lessons; minimise your contact with cruel and aggressive people; be aware of cultural differences when travelling to avoid dangerous situations. Yes, you are a spirit free to roam wherever you want, but it is not always appropriate to throw caution to the wind, driving on the wrong side of the road. Life, if you look, does give you signposts.

The peacock symbolises the ego, which wants to be the best in worldly terms. This involves competition and striving to achieve acclaim and recognition. Competitiveness can ultimately reduce creativity — as the charioteer becomes too involved in keeping tabs on the opposition, inner listening diminishes.

It is important not to become lost in preening, caught up in correct form and outer appearances. Play the game, but remember it is only a game. You are more than your clothes, your job, your marriage, your car, your house. There is no need to avoid these outer adornments — all experiences may be doorways to a greater degree of self awareness. Just keep your eyes and ears open.

The dragon symbolises the enormous energy of creative inspiration, which in some people will be an endless torrent of passionate dreams.

The dragon, like our creative mind, will always be surging ahead. However, the challenge for the charioteer is to take the practical steps which will achieve these dreams. For example, you may have brilliant ideas of building a boat and sailing to the Pacific Islands. You may be able to see yourself so clearly accomplishing this, but first comes the plod, plod, surge, plod of all the work and preparation required.

At times, the dragon will be tugging away at us, trying to drag us into the future. The charioteer must learn to relax, enjoying the journey and appreciating each small achievement — otherwise he may end up loathing the very task he set out to accomplish. Before this happens, take time out to rest under the tree, which retains the fragrance of the Fool, and you will remember your laughter and lightness.

The Chariot is the outer journey — the choices we make about what to do with our energy in the practical world. The

Chariot will reflect the depths of inner journeying, or lack of it. It is possible to use all of life as our teacher, learning from our experiences and allowing situations to become mirrors showing us how we could live more creatively and harmoniously.

Travelling with awareness, we will notice we repeatedly meet with similar situations in different disguises. If we are alert we grasp the opportunity to see past these disguises and recognise the patterns of behaviour which undermine our well-being. These patterns can be like weighty, excess baggage; the more we have, the more our forward progress becomes sluggish and uninspired. This baggage is the information incessantly fed to us about who we are and what is in store for us. Many of us are surrounded by people who subtly or overtly tell us how to be, what we will be good at and suited for and how to rearrange ourselves to fit the mould. Be alert — chew over these messages and spit them out straight away if they don't taste right. Some messages may be very flattering and seductive, so we must constantly check inside to recognise the truth, or more likely the misleading nature, of these declarations.

The charioteer travels lightly. This lightness comes about through self listening and leads to a heightened sensitivity towards other travellers. The power of loving compassion and the power of loving discernment create openness and safe boundaries for the journey. The charioteer ensures that a personal quest is not harming other beings.

The Chariot may be the willingness to take a visible stance on some issue, an outer confirmation of an inner belief. When this stance is in harmony with the Earth, a tremendous sense of well-being arises. Courage has overcome the fear of failure and the outer and inner life are in accord.

It is not all plain sailing for the charioteer. There is the difficulty of living in the marketplace, continuously bombarded through the senses with a kaleidoscope of choices and distractions. The mind loves these distractions and draws all of the noise of the marketplace inside: 'Buy this image now and you'll have all the love, sex, friends and power you want.' The charioteer may become totally sidetracked, deserting what he truly loves to do.

The outer journey is brought into balance through reflection and meditation. We journey within to a still and non-reactive place, where we are able to reflect upon the myriad opportunities which present themselves. Travel with outer eyes and inner eyes seeing simultaneously. Hear the marketplace and hear the wise voice which speaks to you out of the silence. Then you will journey well and travel lightly.

Justice

The image of Justice usually comes to us in a tarot spread when we have awakened to the recognition of some significant state of imbalance. Through the seeing we are unable to remain as passive observers, colluding with the events and evidence before us. The image portrays the state of our planet today, in which technology, by and large, overwhelms rather than enhances ecology. This outward manifestation is also seen reflected inwardly, as the endemic ennui and spiritual famine in which the Western World is engulfed.

A hand holds the scales. This is what is required — the commitment from each of us to make a difference, to take some practical action, no matter how large or small, to rectify the imbalance in whatever way we feel drawn to. In doing so we need to support ourselves lovingly and compassionately, knowing we will not always succeed and knowing we will at times despair of our lack of courage. We need to be aware of our personal limitations and boundaries to help prevent us becoming overwhelmed with the enormity of the continuous breaches in human dignity and environmental well-being.

The image of Justice reminds us that part of any healing journey involves travelling into the darkness — the darkness within ourselves and within our culture. If we remain conscious of this possibility we are less likely to be crushed by the feelings of grief, shame, pain and powerlessness which frequently arise when we seek to redress injustices. Some brave campaigners begin alone, modern-day Davids facing their Goliaths. Most of us need the loving support of a like-minded community to provide the strength required to nourish the vision.

Midnight is the hour shown on the clock face, the time of greatest darkness and also the doorway to the new day. Justice encourages us not to hesitate any longer: by doing the best we are capable of in this moment we offer ourselves to Life itself as another conduit through which transformation may flow.

The Hermit

The Hermit represents the longing of all seekers who yearn for an ever-greater depth of self understanding. This image signifies our withdrawal from all external activities in the world which would label us. It is time to take a break — from work, family, commitments and committees. At times we can only achieve a greater degree of clarity by removing ourselves physically from all the people and situations constantly telling us who we are.

This sense of seclusion is portrayed here by the enveloping nature of the fronds of an ancient survivor from primordial times — the giant tree fern known as the mamaku. The shadows of the night further inform us of the Hermit's withdrawal from any peripheral focus and distraction. The Hermit is in repose — there is no need to assume any spiritual posturing by sitting or kneeling in some uncomfortable way. Easiness and receptivity are present in this body.

The moonlight, reflecting in the pool before the Hermit, shows him no one but himself. However, this is no Narcissus, pining away for love of his own image. The Hermit sees the outer form — and also sees the formless wonder beyond. This illumination is depicted in the shape of the pond, which symbolises the Third Eye, one of the body's energy centres. When the Third Eye becomes active, through meditation and increasing awareness, the veils which have obscured our true perceptions fall away.

When we come to this pool, we will see only our own reflection, no matter who indicated the way for us to arrive at this place. Here is the realisation of gratitude for all our teachers and guides, and also the recognition of our own efforts which have opened our eyes to our own divinity. The goodness and glory we see in another is also a reflection of our own forgotten beauty.

This is often a time of wordless prayer. It is vital to remain alert, as the mind will long to become emotional about this sense of being deeply moved, to tell people, 'I had this amazing experience . . .' In the telling, the moment is lost. Relax: if you are true at this time, the inner voice will speak.

It often happens that the mind immediately wants to create a comprehensible explanation for what is happening in the Hermit experience. Many people who have deeply significant insights, hearing and seeing God within, rush off the next day and join a religious organisation. From this peak moment on, the glorious experiences of wholeness will fall away: illumination always eludes doctrinal and dogmatic containment.

So be aware of the urge within the mind to capture God. It is time to let go of the boundaries created by external contexts of oaths, rituals, initiations and creeds. Experience life exactly as it is — life will speak to you so richly you may never again pick up your Bible, your Koran.

Some may believe you have really lost the path, because of the very simplicity of your wisdom. This is the mystery: only the very wise can live in utter peace and ordinariness. For most others, these truths are merely homilies.

Accept the reality of your experience. The Western World has seduced many of us into believing reality is material visibility.

The Hermit may challenge all previously held beliefs. Thus, the mind may experience an ideological crisis. Trust this process and listen for what is to be heard, beneath all the chatter and clatter of imposed and now crumbling convictions.

An external circumstance may throw you into the Hermit experience: the death of a loved one, the loss of a career, a physical illness, the disintegration of a previously treasured pathway which has become a dead end. Listen beyond the hackneyed condolences and 'in deepest sympathies' as people project onto you their own fears of loss and separation.

The experience of the Hermit occurs at a subtle level which cannot be seen, although the sensitive will be aware of a great energetic change within. Relax into the stillness, delaying the urge to share with others. You are being opened to the glorious treasure within, more exquisite and luminous than you could have ever imagined. Draw closer to this inner light — move towards it with open arms. This is the gift of eternal life and eternal light.

The Wheel of Fortune

At the centre of the Wheel of Fortune is the Third Eye, reminding us of the need to remain alert and aware in our daily lives. To meditate for an hour a day, then blunder on regardless, is not sufficient and chaos will be perpetuated.

A mandala radiates from the Third Eye. Mandalas have been used for centuries, in architecture, art and religious symbols. Meditating on these geometric patterns gives us greater access to the right brain. The left, logical, hemisphere slowly stills, as it cannot deal with the spatial relationships of the mandala, except in an analytical way.

The yellow circumference of the mandala represents the divine clarity available to us when we seek stillness in the midst of chaos. This stillness arises when we see our situation without labelling — this is good, this is terrible, this is God's punishment or God's gift.

On the periphery of this image swirl the events of everyday life, which, unless we remain aware, will give us the exhilaration and terror of a rollercoaster — but our shrieks and groans in response to our emotional reactions will not bring us any great wisdom or insight.

Among the distractions are the elves and witches of fairytale fantasy land. This image portrays our longing to live happily ever after, waiting for our handsome prince or adoring princess, or blaming the ogre — in the form of the boss or the neighbour or the politician — for our misery. Here we believe in fate, not seeing anything we can do to alter our destiny.

Moving clockwise around the image, we see the trunks of great trees, with minimal light penetrating to the forest floor. This segment represents the old adage, You can't see the wood for the trees. Without the light of awareness and insight, we become caught up in petty stances and challenges, investing huge amounts of energy in being right and in winning. Because we can't see the root causes of our actions, we develop elaborate justifications for our behaviour. Under this gloomy canopy are found vast amounts of historical debate, legal sparring, political grovelling and dogmatic assertion, all justifying war, oppression, starvation, and racial and religious hatred.

The next three images symbolise the external roles we play out, for which we may have been indoctrinated and groomed from an early age. These roles tell us how we should appear and to what we should aspire, rather than how to be — how to contact our innate creativity and wisdom.

Just as actors are at risk of becoming over-identified with the character they are currently playing, so are we all susceptible to limiting ourselves through seeing ourselves as the sum total of our key role or roles: I am the Good Provider, the Homemaker, the Rebel, the Politician, the Champion, the Failure, the Conquered, the Altruistic Martyr, the Vengeful.

No matter how great or small the labels — no matter how seemingly powerful or humiliating — we limit our potential when we fully identify ourselves by the labels we have. All these labels will eventually be taken from us; wear them lightly so they will slip off easily.

The image of the person buried in the newspaper represents the constant diet of negativity and despair, atrocities and indignities fed to us each day, until horror becomes numbed resignation. This sense of helplessness causes us to cling, tremulously, to shaky traditions and questionable values.

Look around you. In the midst of the bombardment is beauty, and acts of true unsentimental, unannounced goodness and purity. You will not find them recorded in the newspapers; you will see them by looking afresh at your life and your loved ones, at the sky and the trees. This nourishment will give you the strength to see the pain of the Earth and to become an active participant in the healing.

Finally, the masks portray your hiding of your true face from the world, for fear of being rejected. If you build up years of repressed responses, your face and whole body become rigid and tight. Language is full of these masks: Put on a brave face, Keep your chin up, Turn the other cheek, Smile and the world smiles with you, Turn a blind eye.

The Wheel of Fortune encourages us to see the patterns of

our worldly experiences and to recognise how these patterns are perpetuated through our thoughts and beliefs. A central recognition, rather than a peripheral reshuffle, is what will make the difference to well-being.

It is significant that the image of the Hermit precedes the Wheel of Fortune in the seasonal progression of the Life Songs. The Hermit is the experience of finding a sense of inner stillness and non-reactivity. The Wheel of Fortune challenges this discovery as we are confronted by the kaleidoscope of external events which swirl and shimmer about us. We can remain on the outside in the swirling and believe we are changing, especially if life is crammed with events and we are reacting to drama after drama. This is the veil we need to remove from our eyes — the belief that change is occurring within because change is occurring on the outside.

Our true Centre of Being never changes but, rather, remains as a potent energy source, dormant until we learn to tap into the limitless pool of wisdom. When this connection is made, initially and fleetingly, the seeker will say, 'I have changed so much.' In essence, however, this is not change but a revealing. Masks are removed, false face after false face.

For those who are accustomed to living on the periphery, learning to move to the Centre will initially appear dull — the mind will fight to make a conditioned response. Eventually, as the discipline of watchful, non-reactive awareness continues, we create a haven of tranquillity within ourselves. Initially we have to be very mindful of contacting with this space. Ultimately, we live from this place.

Strength

The mysterious image of Strength has the quality of a transformational dream in which every aspect may be interpreted metaphorically, as a reflection of one's own true inner nature. The Strength card portrays the innate power, beauty and wisdom which arise through the deepening of love.

The proximity and tenderness between the woman and the lion here signify our readiness to relinquish any lingering patterns of conquest and submission, of controller and victim, so often acted out in relationships.

Although the woman is outwardly serene and placid, the lion is a mirror of her inner reservoir of power. Her easiness in the presence of this magnificent beast indicates the understanding and befriending of her passion. This passion is the glorious emergence of our beauty, pouring forth energetically whenever we give ourselves to our love, whether this be a loved one or any act of creativity.

Strength is a paradoxical image which could equally well be named vulnerability. True strength requires self knowledge, trust and the willingness to acknowledge our vulnerability. To be vulnerable does not equate with powerlessness. Vulnerability, as portrayed in the woman's merging with Earth, is the recognition of our dependence upon the planet's well-being for our survival and sanity.

The hues of green — the predominant colour in this image — assure us of our extremely instinctive abilities as healers. Strength informs us that it is appropriate now to offer our gift of insight to others. This may also be the time to commit ourselves to a period of refining and deepening our knowledge in a field relating to health and spiritual well-being.

The incomplete daisy chain symbolises openness to unlimited love; there is always more to give and to receive. Rigid definitions of how we should relate create closed and lifeless boundaries. The flowers also remind us that love must be given life and expression each day. We cannot depend on bygone rituals and promises to guarantee the continuation of love. We must be willing to renew our joy and delight daily, with gratitude.

The presence of the Empress Tree indicates that the blessing of the Great Mother is upon you — follow your heart with commitment and dedication. The courage you need will be at hand, and your instinctive discernment will guide you.

The Hanged One

Do you remember, as a child, hanging upside down from a tree or in an adventure playground? Or putting your trust in an adult as you were held by your feet and walked along on your hands? There was such enjoyment to be found in relaxing the body, feeling the air about you and the sensation of your hair falling away from your scalp. This memory contains the essence of the Hanged One — unbending and allowing a change of perspective, resting in the moment and allowing yourself to resist the mind's demands for goal-oriented activities.

The Hanged One is the experience of a deep sense of surrender, where personality-identification is suspended, allowing us to reach into hidden depths of our strengths and vulnerabilities. When we are able to totally let go into this experience, we feel a blurring of what we usually name Me, and with this comes a sense of merging with everyone and everything around us. Thus the Hanged One may represent a profound moment in our lives and, even though the sensation may be brief, its effect upon us may be lasting.

Many paths lead to this experience; this surrender may come upon us through the conscious practice of becoming fully aware of this present moment, whatever it holds for us. This is the purpose of all meditation practices.

It may come upon us seemingly unelicited. The image of bungy jumping — leaping from a great height to be suspended by elasticated ropes — exemplifies the many thrill-seeking escapades which can, quite unexpectedly, have the effect of tipping us into another dimension. We may move through and beyond fear, into a most extraordinary sense of release. This release may occur in any situation where we are to some extent at the mercy of elemental forces.

The experience of the Hanged One sometimes occurs when we become ill. Perhaps we have been working towards a goal at such a frantic pace that there has been little acknowledgement of the body — the vessel for the journey. The body creates a drama to remind the mind that there is a physical form that must be taken into account. When we are forced to take time out we often examine our priorities from a very different perspective.

Our Western culture is, by and large, obsessed with control. The bridge in this instance represents the structured rigidity of the pre-planned future, with all activities being goal-oriented to ensure we are constantly improving ourselves in worldly terms. This polarised state gives rise to its opposite: a quest for an experience of surrender.

The fading images drifting away in the ebbing tide symbolise the letting go of roles and attachments which now no longer serve our well-being. Thus, the Hanged One symbolises a marked change in the perspective we have about the choices we are making. The Hanged One may be the acceptance of the realities of inhabiting the human body and living within a lifespan. We may give up the warlike attitudes we have towards our frailties and become kinder and gentler towards ourselves. We reflect on the qualitative changes we would like to make in our lives in order to experience a greater degree of health and well-being.

This is a time of learning to love and live with our imperfections. We discover what happens when we pause and listen to ourselves, rather than forcing ourselves onwards relentlessly.

The Hanged One may signify surrendering to the natural rhythms of creative manifestation. We trust that change and the revealing of new directions will come in time. We wait, knowing the moment will arise. In the same way we know that pulling apart the closed petals of a bud means the beauty that would have been is lost forever, so we wait upon the natural unfolding of inspiration. If it is not yet at hand, the Hanged One asks us to allow a fertile receptivity — an openness to receive — to swell within, without expectation.

With the Hanged One, we have the opportunity to move beyond reacting as an emotional pendulum. The opportunity is here for relaxing in the midst of all, in balance and at peace. Life is calling us to pause long enough to discover this place.

Death

The Empress Tree dies and crashes to the Earth. The forest falls silent in the aftermath. Then slowly, slowly, the songs of the forest birds return and the children of the Empress Tree stretch deep into the earth and reach towards the sky.

This image of Death portrays the eternal cycle of life, death and rebirth. This cycle occurs throughout life, as well as at the actual time of departing from the physical body. In fact, life is constantly presenting us with opportunities to totally let go of all that encumbers us, in order for us to fully embrace life with fresh openness.

First examine the Tree herself. The white bark of her trunk and branches signifies the purity and innocence which comes in death. All the layers of personality, all the masks, any lingering falseness, have fallen away.

The rich colours of the roots and their tenacious appearance represent the dichotomy and reluctance that many of us feel at a time of letting go. There is the longing for freedom. And also there is the pain of grief, and attachment to memories, people, possessions and achievements, and the security of the known. This creates the sensation of being wrenched away from the past. The aura of indigo around the Empress Tree expresses the mystical experience we feel when we finally surrender fully to accepting that this is how it is.

The delicate new growth beneath the Empress Tree represents new life emerging from the old form. The seed carries all the wisdom of the tree — and also is given a new and different timespan in which to bring forth the fragrance and fruit of this knowledge. The sapling does not veer away from death. Death is not seen as being divorced from life. Each moment we die to the old and there is a brief gap so that the new can come. The experience of Death is the gap.

The cone of light above the Empress Tree is the transformation of energy which occurs at the time of death or death-like experiences, where the unknown becomes known, and there is the sense of dissolving and union.

The Death card does symbolise endings and beginnings. However, until we acknowledge actual death, then we are unable to see clearly that we are constantly surrounded by the subtleties of conception, birth, life, death and rebirth. The acknowledgement of death does not mean we understand it, but if we live daily with the knowledge that death will occur, then we move from the terror of the unknown towards befriending the mystery.

When actual death is recognised our life choices become richer and fuller. We allow ourselves to flower abundantly. We move away from petty restrictions and guidelines. It is vital we use every opportunity in life to move fully into letting go, consciously and meditatively, examining our responses to the passing of all things — simple daily changes and disruptions.

The Western television culture is utterly pervaded with images of the grossness of death. Perhaps this is representative of a culture's inability to see death as anything but a violation, an indignity, an insult. It remains a relatively rare occurrence for films to depict people who are in harmony with their final hours, people who let go into peace rather than having Death leap forcefully and unexpectedly at them.

Medical science and technology are being used to an even greater extent to manipulate the time of death's arrival, postponing it until the dying becomes a mechanistic obscenity. To die is perceived as failing yet, so often, when people surrender to dying in an atmosphere of deep respect, love and support, it becomes the ultimate experience of healing and completion. Dying is then experienced as a sacred rite of passage.

Fortunately, this tide of negativity towards death is turning, with the work of people such as Elisabeth Kübler-Ross, Stephen Levine and Ram Dass, bringing to the Western World new vision and understanding of this mystery initiation.

Forgiveness plays a major part in allowing us to die to a past we may wish was different — more this, more that. To carry the burden of unresolved griefs is to live a life of suffocating limitations. To forgive ourselves is to die to the chains of suffering. Unless we know how to die to the past — with full gratitude for all we have learnt, and for those we have loved — how can we expect the fragile bud of rebirth to emerge within us?

When something is ending, simultaneously something is being born. We need to move with great sensitivity and awareness. Otherwise, dying to the past becomes an act of violence, and that which is new will not even be recognised.

How we die and how we live are less than a breath apart.

Renewal

Renewal is a cathartic release, a farewell song and a great letting go of something or someone that was once a vital presence in your life. Renewal represents the intermingling of pain, joy and insight, bringing about a sense of being deeply healed. Thus Renewal is the unfolding of the experience of rebirth, begun in Death. The times of Renewal are some of the peak experiences on our journey. We feel an outpouring of gratitude and a glorious affinity with other living beings.

These moments of illumination are symbolised in the Renewal card by the riotous colours of exploding fireworks above the dancers. The blazing fire is fuelled by wood cut from a dead tree, signifying acceptance of the fact that nothing retains its outer form forever. When we are open to life's teachings, we will experience a great furnace within — a ball of flame, burning hot and fast. The truth is like oxygen, feeding the flames until all coarse matter within us — all the dead wood — becomes dust and returns to the earth, and our Being remains as glowing embers purified from fear, anxiety and reactivity.

Ecstasy is channelled through the physical body in dancing, singing and music-making, radiating from one to another, and another — on and on — creating an energy field of thanksgiving. This image also portrays the joyous sense of community which arises when we find ourselves amongst others with whom we feel a strong rapport. We experience our mutual commitment to the path as an energetic wave, carrying us much further than we could travel alone.

Our shadows are present in these festivities; they are here for the healing. Dance, song and music have for centuries been powerful mediums for releasing the pent-up anger, resentment and grief held within the body. Dissolving these tensions, we are able to look more clearly at the truth inside ourselves.

When we give ourselves totally to the dance of life and enter in so fully that we hold nothing back, going beyond previous limits created by a rigid mind, we reach the experience of supreme inner stillness.

The voices rise and fall as each person experiences aloneness and union. No one leads and no one follows; instead a beautiful blending creates a great wholeness. Like each log on the fire, we are separate and yet all come from the one Tree of Life. The children of the Earth Mother are dancing home.

The Devil

The Devil symbolises our reunion with powerful aspects of ourselves which we have previously cast aside as unsavoury and harmful. To see the faces of the Devil, we first have to recognise the fears and myths surrounding this archetype.

The most prevalent teaching about the Devil seems to be this: 'The Devil is outside of you, ready to enter during any moment of inattention on your part. The Devil lurks, always seeking to corrupt and pollute. Idle hands and minds become willing workers for the Devil.' The tarot image demonstrates what happens to us when we try to ignore and hide from an energy we are too terrified to come to terms with.

From a very young age, a division is created within us through all the messages telling us how we should think, feel and act. We lose almost all remembrance of the goodness within our bodies. This sense of rightness and delight becomes muted and corrupted as we become *nice*. Nice is all in the mind: how we think we should relate to people. Rightness is felt as a flame in the belly, a passionate knowledge of what we want and what we know.

This niceness is portrayed in the upper half of the image, with the greeting-card sweetness of sentimental sunlight, which filters through fluffy pink-tinged clouds to light the hills in the distance. The image says, 'Cheer up — the future will be better. Get well soon and, if by chance you pass away, thank God you're saved by belief in eternal life with Jesus.'

When we manipulate our emotions in order only to express niceness, our bodies become fuller and fuller, choking with resentment for all the times we have not listened to the body. When we are so clogged and up to our ears in repressed feelings we are no longer sensitive to the signals the wise body is giving to us.

But, with all this energy of the past stored inside, a coarser shuddering and vibration is set up. The lid lifts as the pressure builds, and our veneer cracks. Emotions erupt, unsolicited. We feel hurt and misunderstood. We may feel guilt and rush to the priest to confess our sins, and the surface will become smooth for a few hours.

Below all this sweetness and light there is an abundance of untapped wisdom. And, because it has not been recognised, it has become totally entwined and strangled with emotions and beliefs, making it very difficult to respond with a sense of clarity to a current situation. For example, if I am angry with my lover but do not consciously deal with the present issue right now, the anger becomes a monster which engulfs and devours us. Any energy to which we cling, refusing to resolve, becomes ugly.

From one small incident, the snake grows. 'He's done this before . . . he doesn't really love me . . . I remember when . . . if only I'd stayed with . . . perhaps my true love will come one day . . . oh, I'm such a bitch . . . why can't I be more like . . . and be more loving, accepting, patient, kind . . . he doesn't know the real me . . . we've become strangers . . . oh (sob) this song reminds me of when we were so happy . . . does love always end up this way . . . I've got a right to punish him . . .' In a matter of seconds another gremlin is given life. To preserve this creature, to wrap it up in guilt and swallow it whole, is a prescription for misery.

We are able to break out of this cycle if we catch ourselves the moment the drama begins — or the moment before, if possible. Most of our dramas follow a set pattern. By being aware of our responses, we are able to release ourselves from repetitive communication breakdowns. We come to know which situations act as a trigger. With this information we can find creative ways to avoid, diffuse or transform events which evoke disturbance. It may also be that through recognising the trigger, it no longer has power over us.

The caricature of the witch symbolises the Wise Ones who have been misrepresented, maligned and murdered, throughout history, by those who do not know God. These phony spiritual teachers create false mysteries to terrorise and control the masses. The priests have burned the manuscripts of ancient knowledge in order to advance their own actions. But they will never totally succeed, because the truth is written within each of us and as we awaken it becomes a living voice, guiding us.

The monsters are stagnant pools of unresolved feelings. We do not necessarily have to go back into the past, reliving the entry and expansion of each of these energies. Life is always sending us opportunities to resolve experiences which once crippled us.

We need to listen to and watch ourselves — when we are alone and when we are with other people — and begin to question. 'Now, where did that idea come from? Is this true in my experience, or did someone just tell me this is so?'

In the image the trap door cannot remain shut. We must look within consciously or we will ultimately become engulfed by this enormously repressed force. The expression of this is seen starkly and horrifyingly in the acts of violence, cruelty and evil perpetrated around us daily in our civilised society, in which we are trained from birth to become rigid and divisive. The befriending of our own monsters is a vital part of the journey to the Centre of Being.

The destructiveness of the Devil occurs when we project all that we have judged as evil in ourselves, and hidden, onto others. We will only ever move to deep levels of Justice when we are courageous enough and can laugh enough to meet with all which has been labelled as darkness.

The split from the Being begins when the child has perceptions that are not seen to be valid, when the child is told, 'You are not hungry . . . you need to sleep . . . I don't want to spoil you.' When children are forced to make loving gestures to people they do not feel love for, this also splits the child's Being.

Perversion and evil result from layers of corruption of the Being — little devils ignored, punished, condemned. So much is shoved into the closet, rather than carefully examined and respected, that there is an enormous accumulation of unresolved energies.

Dis-ease usually has such simple origins, but it becomes ever more complex, tragic and painful when there is a continuing unconscious rejection of the Devil. The Devil grows ever larger in the darkness; the little Devil becomes the big Devil. The more people try to ignore their little Devil, the more internally polarised they become.

With so many people ignoring the Devil, society becomes sick, unwilling to acknowledge any personal responsibility. To ignore the Devil is ultimately to become ugly, bigoted, grasping and pillaging. Recognise and delight in your wickedness — bring the light of clear consciousness and understanding to illuminate the madness of the mind. Laugh and become the witness, observing without attachment. As long as we maintain any piety — 'I am above this, I have moved beyond any flaws' — then the Devil will leap across our path and we will crash down.

Learn to appreciate the rush of energy — anger, rage — that the Devil brings. Feel the surge of this force and see it with full recognition, then choose how to harness this energy. The Destroyer and the Creator are part of the same breath. Breathe deeply.

On exploring the Devil, it is vital to maintain humour, balance and perspective. Many therapies available today go some way in helping us to explore the uncharted terrain of our fears, guilt, hatred and many unresolved, painful experiences. Remain alert, however, because this exploration is full of pitfalls, even with a guide.

For example, people in the role of therapist may have hidden agendas which foster inadequacy and dependency within those who seek counsel. In these situations, wounds are ripped open repeatedly, rather than allowed the illumination of conscious recognition and awareness which heal the internal rifts.

The explorer may also become so fascinated by the inner cauldrons, simmering with pungent emotion, that there may be a distinct reluctance to reach resolution — it might be too boring! The mind easily becomes addicted to the excitement of cathartic experiences. Many people enjoy this feverish intensity and become 'therapy junkies', trying anything and everything in order to find one more excuse to remain unhappy and discontented and to get attention.

The resolution of the conflict portrayed in the Devil card is conveyed by the Tree of Life. When we allow all experiences to become our teachers, we rise above the confusion of contradictory beliefs and incompatible doctrines. We do not mimic any idea of what goodness and love are. We give expression to these qualities when they arise naturally, without any force. We give up inner civil wars, so often fuelled by guilt and self reprisal. True wisdom and maturity flourish.

The Tower

The dramatic image of the Tower may evoke consternation. It is, however, a positive image: it symbolises total release from circumstances which have become constricting and controlling. This card often denotes a situation which we have felt uncomfortable with for a long time, and yet have not adequately addressed. It will become a larger and larger problem, until we are forced to see exactly what is going on.

The Tower represents adherence to belief systems or lifestyles which diminish our well-being. We may find ourselves caught on a treadmill of frantic activities which we know, deep inside, are not what we want to be involved in.

The sea monster, rising from the depths of our unresolved psyches, reminds us of the inevitability of chaos when we ignore too many little disturbances for too long. If we escape to the top of our heads, into the mind, ignoring the wise body, we are merely postponing dealing with the lack of resolve in our lives.

In the eye of the storm there is no easy escape and we must face this crisis. The ominously rumbling sky and the turbulent sea are the Voices of Life calling us to wake up. Yet all is not lost: a tremendous beam of light radiates from the Tower. This symbolises the conscious mind, which has been shaken into full alertness. This is when we say 'Aha!', as the scales of the monster within fall from our eyes and we recognise what we have been doing to ourselves.

It is too late to exit gracefully and to make amends. But, if we allow the light of awareness to penetrate us totally, we experience enormous release and relaxation. In the falling is the healing. The Tower is the Great Awakener. If we are able to see this moment for what it is — the gift of freedom — this will release us from a repetitive cycle of entering into situations which imprison us.

While the Tower usually represents an initially acceptable

situation or relationship which now is experienced as a claustrophobic prison, there are several other meanings which need to be considered. As with all interpretations of imagery, these meanings depend on the placement of this image in a tarot spread and on the question being asked.

The Tower may signify resistance to making a commitment, for fear of tying yourself into something from which it may be difficult to escape. You may already know what is at the base of this perception. If you don't know, this might be a good opportunity to delve deeper and find out.

This resistance is often marked by a continuous uprooting and over-examination of any foundations which are being laid. Superficially, this may appear to be a healthy concern that everything goes well from the beginning. A lot of dust rises, with negotiations, asking for second opinions and other stalling strategies. It is soon obvious (if not to yourself, then at least to the people around you) that delaying tactics are being used.

Apprehensions of this nature often occur in new relationships, after an initial period of falling in love. One or both people begin to ask themselves, 'What if I go much further, and then find out this is not what I want to do? Is this the person I am really destined to be with?'

However, through consciously recognising and naming your fears about commitment, you are in a much better position to create foundations in a relationship which have a more harmonious basis than you have previously experienced.

The Tower at times signifies that you are responding with alertness and clarity to circumstances which would have previously thrown you off balance. You have consciously changed your approach and, in doing so, the elements of drama and upheaval are greatly diminished. You move more fluidly through difficulties, realising you do have choices about how you react.

The Star

The Star signifies the call from the wise and gentle spirit which lives within each of us. We are asked to undertake our life learning with great compassion, forgiveness and kindness towards ourselves. We need this moderating and tolerant attitude to assimilate whatever intense and illuminating experiences the Tower has brought to us.

The Star represents a mystical experience of balance. We do not need to approach the divine through first attempting to purify ourselves of those aspects we deem to be unacceptable — perhaps such qualities as jealousy, greed, anger and withholding of love. Rather, we consciously bring our frailties and failings with us, blending all the lost and outcast parts of ourselves together with our own exquisite beauty, creativity and goodness.

The sunlight creates rainbows by reflecting off the flaws within a crystal. This is the beauty which is discovered with the Star, when we bring all of who we are to our spiritual quest. The Star symbolises the visionary who has healed herself to a degree whereby she is now able to show others how to release the jewel within themselves.

The Star is the integration of the physical with the metaphysical. The Star Woman's glorious gown of fire-threads and silver moonbeams enshrines the Earth. She harmonises spiritual yearnings with practical endeavours, ensuring that the pursuit of one is not to the detriment of the other.

We may experience long periods of aloneness during our Star search, and yet also be aware of an encompassing sense of protection. In the background of the Star image we see pyramids of Egypt and the sacred natural monument of Australia, Ayers Rock, here representing the wisdom of the ancient Wise Ones. Although so much esoteric knowledge has been lost to us, we are able to regain its timeless essence by using the light of our own understanding to teach us.

The Moon

The Moon is the interplay of muted light and silvery water or of shadows and murky depths. It all depends upon your perspective.

The sea creatures seen here symbolise the wisdom contained deep within the unconscious, which is most often told to us through our dreams. The crab coming ashore indicates the emergence of ancient knowledge, always contained, though frequently unrecognised, within us. It is vital here to stay alert and free from emotional reactivity. When truth is illumined within, the mind wants to find a category into which to slot this experience. On first 'seeing the light', the mind will decide this is Jesus, or Krishna, or Buddha speaking. Or the mind may decide the wisdom is from some disembodied spirit which has chosen this living body to be its medium.

While there are voices in the spirit world that may speak to us, we need to be aware in the first instance that each of us has a wise, guiding spirit within us. When we open to the possibility that this wisdom has always existed within us, we become aware of a huge well of strength, available to be drawn upon. Some religious paths teach us that this strength only exists outside of ourselves. This creates a great vulnerability within us as we are then required to align ourselves with an external voice of God, whose messages may at times run contrary to the direction in which we innately feel drawn.

The crab beckons us to journey closer to the source of Light. The image depicts a pathway created by the turtles' backs, and these aquatic reptiles reassure us the way is ancient and yet vitally alive. These living stepping stones have been used many times before.

The fins and tails (of who knows what?), breaking the mill-pond stillness of the sea, remind us of the mind's disquiet and desire to distract us from putting one foot in front of the other. Life will always send events which may ruffle the surface. The mind wants to leap into the jaws of emotional dramas, to be gobbled up, to experience violent sensations — anything to avoid moving towards silence and peace.

The sandcastle in the foreground reminds us that the shifting sands of worldly achievements — all monuments, all outer forms — will eventually crumble and be washed away. This knowledge helps us to move into the unknown, when we experience impermanence where once there was stability and dependability.

The zigzagging pathway through the hills indicates our ever-heightening ability to address life issues with clarity. Each time a similar situation comes along we see more quickly what is happening. The two peaks represent the heightened understanding of love, whereby we are able to each stand alone without loneliness and, therefore, experience union and harmony with loved ones without any clinging and sentimentality. We refuse to remain as molehills of emotional dependency and manufactured needs, recognising that we are really mountains.

The Moon herself is the essence of receptivity to the mystery of love. The shadows created by her light are the dark corners within ourselves. Do not become waylaid exploring dingy niches. So many people spend so much time sparring with shadows. Just see the pathway in the moonbeams. Moving towards the light, we find all else is diluted and dissolved.

The Moon is an uncomfortable card for those who like to walk the rational, logical, ten-year-plan path. The Moon indicates strongly that now is the time when the future will not be revealed to us with sharp definition and clarity. All that can be done is to trust this next step; the moonlight will reveal this much. We only think, 'It's too dark — I can't see' because of the initial difficulty in adjusting to seeing what is right before us. The moonlight offers us this gift. In the light of day, we can see great distances, and so there is often a failure to look closely at what is around us: relationships and health crumble while we are on the goal-quest.

The experience of the Moon is one verging on panic: 'I feel so confused.' The left brain may be in confusion — in anger. It is time to relax, meditate and visualise, and commit our concerns to our dreaming time. The Moon calls us to heighten our intuitive responses — the responses which come so easily to the Fool, but which may have been lost or diminished through lack of use and trust.

Follow the cycles of the moon and make time to observe the night sky. If you live in the city, try to spend some evenings in the country. Lie on your back and open your eyes to the splendour, enormity and mysteries above you. In a state of relaxation and surrender, you will come to understand and be at peace with the soft focus of nocturnal luminousness.

The Moon is the womb of intuition and spiritual knowledge. For those who listen with certainty to their inner voice there is no need for external counsel or confirmation.

The Sun

After groping our way, trusting, and perhaps wavering, step by step, in moonlight and darkness, we are rewarded for our courage and tenacity. The new day is born, bringing warmth and clarity. A fresh vitality and resoluteness flows through us. The Sun signifies a time when life blesses us. This blessing is often showered after a prolonged period of testing experiences which have forced us to face our fears and limitations. Through meeting with our frailties, we name the previously nameless ghosts and monsters of our psyches. Knowing and reclaiming these lost parts of ourselves gives rise to compassionate love.

At the centre of this image is a cross contained within a circle. The circle represents the wholeness which arises through the ability to tap into a well-spring of self love. The delightfully energetic and intuitive spontaneity of the Fool is combined with mature self understanding. This knowledge is acquired through living life fully — unblinkered — and seeing all the flaws and imperfections of humanity without becoming distanced and cynical.

The cross signifies the integration of freedom and love, of aloneness and relating. It is likely that significant relationships are extremely satisfying and mutually supportive, without being rigid or necessarily having conventional sanction and definition. You have in your life the people you want around, without any apology or need to please others through your choices.

Creativity becomes a consistent theme in your daily expression. You feel the desire to light up all aspects of your life with aesthetic touches, and to take care with the smaller, as well as the larger, expressions of your life; you may love to prepare beautiful meals, give handmade gifts or create a vivid and fragrant garden.

The Moon, illuminated by the Sun, here reminds us that nothing is black or white: night and day are not forceful opponents, but part of an endless cycle of revealing and shadowing. Thus, we find ourselves having less strong emotions and attitudes on many issues about which we may once have had vehement convictions. We can see the overall ebbing and flowing of life without swinging cathartically high and low in response. We feel an inner constancy.

The Sun, both rising and setting, is contained within this image. The rising Sun signifies the surge of energy which is freed within us when we accept the newness of this day — this moment — and unclutter ourselves from situations which oppress our expression of love and creativity. It is time to reach for our dreams and remove the limits from our ideas about what is possible or impossible.

The multi-hued sky, lit by the setting Sun, represents the repleteness and contentment we feel when we have given ourselves fully to the day, without hankering for any other time or daydreaming wistfully of the past.

The rising and setting Sun also portrays the need to look without and look within, with the same relaxed easiness of breathing — taking what we observe in the world and reflecting this against our understanding of what is right for us.

The open petals of the radiant sunflower encompassing the image symbolise the exuberance with which we meet people and situations. This open receptivity gives each day a fresh aliveness, with nothing viewed as humdrum and monotonous. We are conscious now of weaving the tapestry of our own lives and we are able to recognise which strands, interwoven, will further awaken and express our creativity.

Beyond Judgment

The Judgment card of many traditional tarot decks depicts an image of the dead rising from their graves, awaiting God's final estimate of their worthiness and, therefore, their ultimate fate.

In *Songs for the Journey Home* we recognise the potential for transforming past unconscious actions and painful and dark experiences. Through the process of making peace with our frailties — those aspects of ourselves which we hide away as they seem blemished and defective — we enter into a far greater dimension of compassionate understanding and humility.

By renaming this card Beyond Judgment, we are alerted to the need to move beyond over-categorising and labelling experiences. In the process of trying to comprehend the significance of something which has moved us greatly, it may be reduced to its component parts and the mystery is lost.

The egg which contains the bird and the anchor reminds us we are continually involved in a process of rebirth, breaking out of old and secure patterns when we have outgrown the limits of our previous ways of thinking, perceiving and valuing. The egg also alerts us to be sensitive to natural cycles and rhythms of spiritual growth. We may need known boundaries and a time of emotional incubation before surging forward into new domains. Periods of reflection and assimilation are necessary safeguards in the process of transformation.

The bird represents the flight towards freedom, away from restraints of conditioning and social, religious and cultural expectations. The bird is the authentic beauty we sense when we spread our wings and rise above circumstances which have previously impeded us.

The anchor symbolises experiences which initially appear to weigh us down. These are the hard lessons which bring us down with a bump and cause us to reappraise issues of personal safety which we may have overlooked. The anchor is sometimes experienced as having a cynical and jaded outlook, because of hurts and hard knocks. The anchor is ultimately seen as a symbol of a strong and resilient integrity, with the ability to hold fast in storms and turbulence. In shifting winds and waters we remain true to ourselves.

The hands reach out, simultaneously touching waves of light and dark. We move beyond the surety of rigid perceptions of right and wrong and of why experiences come to us in the ways they do. We are able to see pain and beauty, loss and blessings, intermingle and interweave. We sense patterns which we may not be able to name.

The Homecoming

The Homecoming symbolises the culmination of a series of events and experiences which lead us to a greater degree of at-homeness within ourselves. We see with increasing clarity the blend of metaphysical realities behind everyday physical forms.

The image of the Homecoming tells a mythical story of our life's path on Earth.

We come from the Stars. Although the Star life is a perfect and glorious life, we are unable to recognise its wondrousness as we have never known anything else. As we gaze down at Earth, we hanker for some time in this adventure playground.

We beg our Star Grandmother to let us go, but she always denies us our request. This creates a determination within us. Of course, Star Grandmother knows this is the way it will be. Every dawn, just before Star Grandmother goes to sleep, she uncoils her braided hair. She pretends to sleepily close her eyes and, in this moment, a few of us climb down her tresses, which reach to the Earth. We enter the shell of the physical form.

We come to Earth with the Star light in our eyes. As adults, we love to look deep into a newborn baby's constant and steady eyes. A tremendous sense of peace comes over us, as the spirit within us responds to an unconscious memory.

In the shell of the physical body we are swept along by the Wave of Life. At first we have no understanding of the Wave, and we feel tossed and buffeted without any sense of its intrinsic rhythms. Throughout lifetimes, we come to realise the ebb and flow of the Wave's pulsations. We learn to swim with the currents, rather than battling them. The sounds of the Wave are no longer an indecipherable cacophony of boomings and gurgles. The Wave carries the voice of the Star Grandmother and we learn to discern her words.

The voice of the Star Grandmother is spoken softly within each of us. The more we come to know her voice, the more we have a sense of coming home, no matter what our circumstances in the physical world. Her voice creates a bridge. This bridge is a safe pathway into the dimensions of the spiritual world, while we inhabit the body. The bridge is also the pathway we walk, with the joy of familiarity, when we eventually leave the body at the time of physical death.

The ecstatic moments of life occur when we dance on this bridge: when we experience both dimensions — the physical and the spiritual — simultaneously. In these moments, we are again filled with the Star light. We understand the purpose of this earthly walk and we also know the place to which we will return.

Star Grandmother speaks.

'This is one of the greatest of human endeavours: to build bridges to link the world of the known to the infinity of the Great Unknown Everpresent Beyond.

'Some have been asked to build visible bridges — to take an obvious stance and speak loud and strong, to devote their lives with intensity to delivering a message. And this outpouring of the inner fire will roar and blaze.

'Some have been asked to build invisible, intangible bridges — delicate webs each made anew to assist in the transformation of a specific individual in need of guidance towards their own Star light. To be an invisible guide is to wear the mask of ordinariness — in clothes, in speech, in abode, in eating and drinking — taking on all the gifts and all the trials of inhabiting the body without fighting or resistance.

'In this way, through understanding life in the body so fully, we use it as a bridge into the Mysteries. If we ignore the body, it is all too easy to plunge into the psychic seas, swimming away from the known so completely that we are at risk of becoming totally lost, sucked down into the deep, uncharted underworld caverns. When we find a bridge — when we are a bridge — there is safety in the journeymaking, and we are able to experience multiple realities simultaneously.

'Sometimes we are able to be a bridge for ourselves. At other times we need a guide who can show us how to experience these moments. The guide shows us how to bridge the gaps, the chasms, the dark, deep spaces, so that we become more adept at dancing in both the physical and spiritual realms without becoming trapped in psychic tricks which have no transformative qualities.

'We recognise when life calls upon us to use our strength to defend, to be accountable, to stand firm and to let our truths be known. Listen to the inner voice which guides and you will know when to remain silent and watch. Many people will not acknowledge the visible bridge, and so the invisible path is subtly presented. There must be no blowing of trumpets, for this will startle the traveller, causing wariness. The invisible bridge is subtle — the subtlety of compassionate love, which is the most powerful source of courage. The invisible bridge is not defined by group identification or religious allegiance. It has a vibration — a song for the journey home; so many harmonies flowing together bridge the gap between the dimensions of physical and spiritual realities.

'Life sends so many experiences which are bridges. We need to be slow in judging the rightness or wrongness of any given circumstance. The wholeness of the truth which lies behind an event is often beyond our immediate vision.'

PART THREE
THE SHELL SONGS

AN OVERVIEW

of the Shell Songs

The Shell Songs are mirrors of the roles we play out in
our lives. Each role, entered into consciously, offers us
an expanded view of ourselves. These sixteen cards are
traditionally named the Court cards — pages, knights,
queens and kings. Here they are renamed the Shell Songs,
representing as they do the outer roles we take on to create
the multitudinous experiences available to us in our
physical form.

We are most often satisfied when we are able to move
fluidly between roles, easing out of one and into the next as
is appropriate to the circumstances. We also experience a
deep level of balance and harmony when our outer roles
express our inner creative urges and sense of purpose.

We are most often pulled off balance when we are over-
identified with a particularly dominant role, and ignore or
disown other roles. Even if it is a role we enjoy we may
become weary and disenchanted when we only draw a sense
of accomplishment from one aspect of our lives.

The metaphor of the shell reminds us these roles can be
protective masks. We need to recognise when this
protection is serving our well-being and when it is limiting

the depth of contact we experience with ourselves and those around us. Sometimes our shell grows as we grow and other times we may need to leave a familiar and comfortable shield behind.

Pages have been renamed and are called Innocence. These cards depict our naive, vulnerable, highly instinctive and joyfully inquisitive responses to life.

Knights are named Awakening, and represent the highly charged, potentially zealous and rigid enthusiasms often associated with adolescence.

Queens are named Creating, and represent the mature ability to appreciate dreams and aspirations, and to actively commit to their unfolding into rewarding realities.

Kings are named Resolving, and represent the attainment of wisdom. Here, compassionate recognition of personal strengths and weaknesses brings a tremendous sense of self acceptance.

Throughout the Shell Songs the imagery is equally female and male. Innocence and Creating images are of female children and mature women. Awakening and Resolving images are of male youths and mature men. However, this gender balance is not designed to denote certain attributes as intrinsically masculine or feminine. Each card is applicable as a mirror of a personal experience.

The four elemental qualities of air, earth, water and fire are the key themes of these cards:

Wind Innocence, Awakening, Creating and Resolving all reflect ideas, intelligence and the way our mental attitudes affect our choices.

Earth Innocence, Awakening, Creating and Resolving all reflect our desire to create a physical environment which feels both expressive and protective.

Wave Innocence, Awakening, Creating and Resolving all focus on our emotional world and the degree to which we are able to nourish ourselves and to create satisfying relationships.

Flame Innocence, Awakening, Creating and Resolving all portray our search for creative expression, which is aligned with our sense of spirituality and manifests our appreciation for life in all its forms.

When determining the overall theme of each card, we may look at the elemental energies in the following manner:

All Innocence cards, no matter what their given element, also share the qualities of water. These cards depict malleability, flexibility and the potential to be easily led or persuaded.

All Awakening cards share the ever-changing and elusive characteristics associated with air. These images focus on the mind — its coolness, its trickiness and its intelligence.

All Creating cards express the spirit of earth and the physical efforts needed to give birth to new aspects of our selves and our lives.

All Resolving cards reflect fire, both blazing bright and smouldering embers. Here we come to accept and enjoy our own nature and let go of competing with others, or striving to mimic and conform.

When the Shell Songs come up in readings they show us areas of ourselves which we need to become more aware of, or roles we are acting out which may be undermining or diminishing us. We also need to acknowledge when people in our lives are taking on roles we could well fulfil for ourselves.

Innocence cards may show us where we are being too childish (rather than child-like), passive or impulsive. They can remind us to take better care of ourselves and not to take everyone at face value. We learn to use wisdom in choosing who we reveal our vulnerabilities to, lest further hurt is brought to the inner child.

Awakening cards ask us to pause and reflect before rushing headlong into a new situation. We are reminded to assess and utilise our talents and simultaneously to respect the rights and dignity of other people, who may have made very different choices based on alternative viewpoints. We need to ask ourselves, 'Am I choosing this for the thrill of it, or am I seeking a more lasting experience?'

Creating cards remind us to question the obstacles we assume are keeping us from happiness. At times we limit ourselves through fears and procrastination and may find that, secretly, we are a bit too lazy to make the effort; it's easier to make excuses.

Resolving cards ask us whether we are truly content. Sometimes we achieve our dreams and then realise there is more to be strived for, or a new avenue is opening up to us. We know so much — are we willing to risk the unknown again?

You may find it useful to choose one of these cards each week and to meditate upon the image. Write about how you want to enhance this aspect of yourself. Choose cards which remind you of friends and acquaintances. Recognise the gaps: there may be people you long to have in your life and you may not have been aware of your need. You may want to play with a friend's child, spend more time talking with your mother, or learn a craft or skill from someone whose work you've admired.

Perhaps you are surrounded by such wise, grown-up and serious people that you recognise the need for some frivolous, lighthearted company. Or you may realise you have, for too long, been the great provider of love and physical comfort and want to receive back some of this nurturing instead of focusing on others.

Let the images gently show you your abundance.

Earth Innocence

Earth Innocence is the child who is happiest amongst living, growing beauty. A garden, a park or a beach becomes a wonderful kingdom of fantasy for her. She is aware of the spirit of each plant and creature and feels a great concern for their well-being. She learns about the endless cycles of living and dying through watching the seasons change and conducting funerals for dead birds she finds.

Earth Innocence is a purposeful child who is independent from an early age. She may experience herself as being quite different from other children around her and she knows she thinks and sees differently from most adults she meets.

She has a strong need to be creatively involved with life. Earth Innocence will not wait for expert advice and instead devises often very complex projects for which she may have no prior skill. Moving a step at a time, she has no fear of the task at hand being too large for her.

This image is of a child who has been nurtured by people who have protected her from commercial bombardment — the 'If you have this you will be happy!' message fired at television audiences in every programme break.

When the child is not told what should make her happy, but discovers this for herself, she is free of the need to squeeze herself into an ill-fitting mould.

Earth Awakening

Earth Awakening depicts a young man, on top of the world, whirling with all the potential he senses inside himself and all the possibilities he sees outside.

This image has some of the qualities of the Wheel of Fortune. Earth Awakening may have a chaotic and giddy feeling as he faces numerous opportunities, each of which seem to lead to very different places. Or, like the Sufi dancer, he may hold a point of stillness and trust the voice which speaks to him from this silence.

The uncertainty of this period may be intensifed if Earth Awakening's true choice lies in the opposite direction from the aspirations which significant people in his life have for him.

The image depicts a grand staircase with the red carpet rolled out. This is the option of following in family tradition, where influence and money assure him of a relatively smooth transition into a steady career.

The sweeping, curving path by the pond symbolises a choice which will allow him to use his aesthetic ability in his work. This may involve manual tasks which keep him close to nature.

The cave represents work which will draw on his fascination with the body-spirit connection. Here he will look at working closely with people in some healing capacity.

A golden ray of light flashes around Earth Awakening's body. This is the perfect time to look at all your options, understanding the influences behind each choice. Follow your 'gut reaction' and you will land on your feet.

Earth Creating

Earth Creating radiates effervescent vitality. Her surroundings overflow with visible evidence of her all-embracing approach to life. This is the woman who wants to have it all and often succeeds. She is unperturbed by the disorderly jumble which is the result of her many enthusiasms. She has a certain perennial stability beneath a vacillating appearance.

Earth Creating is a devoted lover, friend, homemaker, champion of environmental causes and generally one of the great workers of the world. She will often rise up as a protector of weak and vulnerable people and thus may make her way into the political arena.

Occasionally she collapses with exhaustion and realises just how many ways she is dividing herself. Sometimes she needs a close friend to remind her to take a break. When Earth Creating is persuaded to have some time out, she does it thoroughly, taking the telephone off the hook and generally making herself unavailable. She will then spend hours reading, gardening or completing a gorgeous garment she began sewing months ago.

However, before tranquillity becomes inertia, she will ask a dozen people to her home for a meal and the bath will be left to overflow again and the whole cascading madness will begin once more.

Earth Resolving

Earth Resolving represents success and celebration of achievements in the material world. He has a generous disposition and loves to share the rewards of his hard-won good fortune. At best he is a philanthropist who genuinely delights in providing the means whereby people with talents but without the financial wherewithal may achieve their dreams.

Because Earth Resolving is mostly identified with external accomplishments, he may be providing for the physical well-being of his loved ones to the detriment of their emotional needs. If there is a major disturbance on the physical level, such as the loss of good health or of a job, this may cause a huge upheaval and lead to a time of questioning and re-examining of values and priorities.

Earth Resolving is likely to have strong and traditional beliefs. While these may create a sense of security and dependability, he may also have expectations which his family, friends or employees cannot live up to. Earth Resolving may be thrown into turmoil when his children have quite different plans for their lives than he had envisaged, and he wonders where he went wrong. It is at times a slow and painful process for him to realise he does not have the ownership of other peoples' destinies.

While he may grapple with issues of power and control, Earth Resolving nevertheless has endearing and redeeming qualities. He is a true life-and-soul-of-the-party type and a great raconteur, hilariously weaving fact with fiction. Often well read and well travelled, he is rarely a bore.

Flame Innocence

Flame Innocence is the child's first spiritual awakening, when she realises there is much more to life than the world she sees with her physical eyes. We see her somewhat cowering from this experience, as there is no one to guide her in the realms beyond the material plane. The child in Western culture is most often left to her own devices, as far as spirituality is concerned, or else loaded up with doctrine and dogma from an early age.

This image has some of the qualities of the Moon card, as the child creates a path for herself through the darkness. Myths and fairytales may be the best teachers for her right now. The flickering candle on her table indicates her recognition of her own divine place on earth.

As an adult Flame Innocence may have lived for years without any perception of divine purpose in her life. Events, which are perhaps crises, may serve to wake her up. This is often a fearful and uncertain time and she may feel like a babe lost in the woods. She may experience an acute sense of separation from the path she has taken up to this time and a period of isolation may ensue.

The time spent alone will create a vacuum into which will be drawn the people and the experiences she needs to draw her to a place of firmer footing.

Flame Awakening

Flame Awakening has discovered the world of knowledge. He is passionately consuming all the information he can, from every person and place that may hold the skill and understanding he hungers for. He may have a mentor who inspires and encourages him.

Flame Awakening often signifies the beginning of a new career or the start of a prolonged period of study. He may have had to work extremely hard to arrive at this new starting point.

We see him standing before so many doors, so many possibilities. Above him hangs an intensely bright light bulb, the beams of which obliterate the soft moonlight outside. For a time he will believe all he has to do to conquer the unknown is to apply himself to arduous study and research.

However, Flame Awakening is a sensitive spirit and behind every known, he discovers another mystery. If he continues to be open to these glimmerings, he arrives at a place where questions cannot be answered. This is where true contemplation and meditation begin.

Flame Creating

Here we see two aspects of the woman who is Flame Creating. The weaver has a quiet constancy, like the embers of a fire which glow through the night. Her inspiration fuels her dreams, even though their unravelling may take years of unseen work and dedication.

In the tapestry she weaves, Volcano Woman is erupting. With the look of operatic intensity, she erupts out of the blue to sing herself into being.

The icebergs in the background of the image depict a cold and bleak environment. Flame Creating does not dissipate too much of her creativity by concerning herself with the lack of receptivity towards her work from the world at large.

Rather than using words, Flame Creating allows her artistic medium to speak for her.

Flame Creating is also the ancient Goddess wisdom — a fire which has never been completely stamped out. Although so much ancient knowledge has been lost, you will rekindle the essence of her many expressions by weaving a creative web throughout each day and into your dreaming time. Give expression to the obstacles in your way. Through singing, dancing, storytelling, poetry and painting, you bring together the threads of your life story and see the gloriously interwoven hues as patterns emerge.

Flame Resolving

Flame Resolving is depicted here as a skilled craftsman who knows his tools and his medium so well he appears to work effortlessly and intuitively.

Flame Resolving is the realisation of one of the dreams of Flame Innocence, through training, persistence and dedication. The ease with which he works leads people to say, 'You're so lucky to be artistic and to work at what you love to do!' At this he will smile wryly, as he knows luck has little to do with the degree of achievement and satisfaction he has.

As well as arousing envy, he will also be an inspiration. Flame Resolving is not daunted by critics' pronouncements and attempts to define his work. He is unconventional and loves experimenting with new methods. He takes risks as he is not controlled by fears of failure.

Each creation has a unique quality of enduring beauty. Here we see jugs, glasses, bowls and vases, all seeming to dance with the interplay of sunlight. Even the most utilitarian of containers has aesthetic touches.

Flame Resolving's life is pervaded with this ability to draw magic into the mundane. He notices the small delights which often pass other people by. He will see the plumage of birds and the shimmering of butterfly wings as opportunities to fuel his imagination. Thus, in some intangible way, he breathes life into each of his creations.

Although he may work in a solitary way, he is also gregarious by nature and loves the company of friends who also have a passionate focus in their lives.

Wave Innocence

Wave Innocence is the youngest and most vulnerable of the People images. Floating in a huge clam shell on a tranquil sea, she reminds us of a time before the natural instincts and reactions are socialised out of the child. So often the child is trained away from self trust and natural abilities.

Wave Innocence marks the return and the deepening of trust in perceptions. The heart can feel the intentions of all hearts and make choices to keep destructive people away. The heart calls close those who encourage you to create a life which flows with your own nature and talents.

This is a dreaming time — a pre-creative time, where ideas ripen, apparently untended. Wave Innocence often seems to be doing nothing, except gazing at clouds, watching patterns in the sand made by the incoming tide and becoming mesmerised by the gardens of kelp swaying in perpetually shifting currents. Leave well alone, because this is how the creative mind does its work — or its play. Wave Innocence never approaches anything head-on, and so you may turn away in frustration. Yet, when you turn back, in the time it took you not to notice, some magic has occurred.

Wave Awakening

Wave Awakening loves to dive deep into love — and lust! — again and again. The searching, the finding and the consummating hold the excitement and fascination. After the conquest is made, interest diminishes and passion dwindles.

The other person desperately wonders, 'What have I done?' What you have done is allowed yourself to become real, known, available and wholly human, rather than remaining a tantalising fantasy, aloof and distant. This love affair lasts longest when both play the game.

Wave Awakening can be a delightful companion for a time, as he is initially charming and romantic. However, you may soon long for a degree of true warmth and intimacy which is not available here.

If you are embracing these qualities of Wave Awakening in your life, you may find eventually you have an empty feeling inside, yet a fear of any commitment. Falling in love with love is wonderful drug. Falling in love with a real and fallible mortal gives you the unforgettable taste of a nectar which transforms your understanding of love forever.

Wave Creating

Wave Creating depicts both the contained and the abundantly overflowing qualities of mature woman. The cliffs curve to create a vase — or perhaps a womb — becoming a vessel into which creativity may be poured, until it overflows. Wave Creating is the wise woman who knows she needs time to replenish herself through periods of retreat and re-evaluation. Here she finds a sanctuary in which it is safe to meet with her feelings and emotions. In a simple ritual she lovingly cleanses herself and reconnects more strongly with her intuitive and sensuous nature.

When she has thus restored her strength her true nature becomes visible. For long periods of time she may appear to have an indefatigable amount of support, tenderness and insight to give. She is the friend who stands firm beside you when you are experiencing an overwhelming crisis. However, be aware if you are becoming too dependent on Wave Creating, for she will sense it too. While she will love you through troubled times, she cannot bear stagnant pools of prolonged misery and self-perpetuated cycles of angst. She may need to withdraw from you in order to take care of herself and to free you to recognise your own strength.

Wave Creating urges us to return to an honest expression of feminine feeling. Many women have been socialised away from clear reactions and responses, becoming manipulative, berating, weak, cute and helpless and, thus, disempowered.

The iridescent dance of the rainbow and the waterfall portrays the vibrancy with which Wave Creating meets the events in her life. Seemingly ordinary moments take on a sparkle. The extreme seriousness with which some approach their day has her smiling to herself. While she has the capacity to be deeply moved, she is also delightfully irreverent and quickly bursts any bubbles of pomposity which may be floating around.

Wave Resolving

This image represents mature love. The arms gently encircling the sea to create a tranquil harbour symbolise the ability to lovingly enfold another without grasping or possessiveness. There is no attempt to change the beloved. Relationship becomes a beautiful resting place; the coming together is a restoring and revitalising time.

The image also represents self understanding, acceptance and contentment. The feeling of love is with you, whether a loving partner is physically present or not.

The little row-boat resting on the sands at low tide indicates the ability to recognise when aloneness is needed. You sensitively respond to your inner tidal flows, knowing when it is right to move towards the other, and when space to yourself is necessary.

The violet and turquoise aura around this Being has a wave-like quality, signifying the letting go of expectations you have imposed on yourself or allowed others to foist upon you. Your openness to examining attitudes and values means you are not significantly swayed by mainstream conformity, although you may lightly integrate into some aspects of the dominant culture around you. Here is relaxation: no struggle any more to justify or clarify, and to explain the choices you have made.

This person may find himself alone, as he is content to wait until the right relationship manifests, with someone who will give and receive love with an equal degree of maturity and insight.

Wind Innocence

Here we meet with the delightful, bubbling enthusiasm of a person rich in plans, schemes and ideas, each one seemingly too large and perhaps too fanciful to achieve. Wind Innocence is not aware of any constraints, seeing the open horizon as a canvas on which to paint dreams.

However, this exuberant character will encourage many to be involved with her numerous projects. These willing servants will find they have taken over all the mundane aspects of each venture, as the intricate precision needed to achieve a goal is too painstaking for this colourful one.

There is the fleeting experience of seeing a butterfly, being with this person and her beauty and freedom, too elusive and intangible to ever be pinned down. Although Wind Innocence has a wide circle of friends, there are few who can say they really know her.

She has a certain egocentrism which can be either charming or frustrating. You will have to decide for yourself which — the butterfly will have fluttered on before you've had time to discuss the problem.

Wind Awakening

Wind Awakening strides headlong into his future. So set is his focus he is oblivious to the effect he has on anyone or anything which happens to be on the same path — there may be a sense of recoiling or else facing the risk of being trampled on!

This image is of someone with passionate beliefs — some may say dogmatic, arrogant and pushy. There is the flavour of the new convert: to an idea, a religion or a political stance. With the newness is an untested, idealistic rawness — the rough edges are all very evident. Wind Awakening is fine in the company of those of a similar persuasion, but he may become tedious and intolerable in the presence of people who challenge, question or simply choose to do things differently.

A wild beauty is also present in this image. Wind Awakening may come to know more of who he is by choosing to dramatically break with the past in order to have an experience of the new. However, at this stage he is somewhat off-beam in his zealous pursuits. Usually he only realises in retrospect the degree to which he has blundered over sacred and precious realms; at some stage on our path home most of us trample on roses without realising what is at our feet.

Because of the intensity of Wind Awakening's aspirations, he has a quality of magnetic attraction and we see the most unlikely people in his company. He is bold, brash and delightful at times, but never, ever, invisible or inaudible.

Be very cautious with your heart around Wind Awakening. If you come from an unloving past, you are particularly vulnerable to continuing to choose people who cannot give you what you need and yet you may spend years begging for the glimmerings of affection.

Wind Awakening may superficially appear to be an appealing challenge, as he may be so aloof, self contained and unmoved. It can be very tempting to think, 'I will be the one to make the difference in this person's life.' In fact, many love stories are written with this theme. Reality rarely has the glowing finale of the novel, however. You are taking a great risk with your happiness, waiting for Wind Awakening to reveal the exquisite gem you know exists deep within him. We are all beautiful at the centre of our Being — be with someone who can share this essence with you now, rather than having it on the ten year plan.

Wind   Creating

Wind Creating takes flight on the back of a huge albatross — a symbol of the strength found in aloneness. She leaves the known cliffs behind; these craggy precipices have perhaps become more of a prison than a protective buttress.

For a person who has become lost in unfulfilling relationships, Wind Creating heralds a time of breaking free from emotionally driven choices. You may need to physically remove yourself from a situation in order to gain a more farsighted perspective about the choices you have. Wind Creating depicts the gap which often exists between the end of one phase and the beginning of the next, and it may be a painful time of breaking with the past while not knowing what the future holds.

People close to you may be dismayed on seeing attributes and longings you have which have been hidden before now. At this time you irrepressibly put your needs ahead of other considerations, and may make what appear to be sudden, rash and irrevocable changes — in career, in living situations, in creative endeavours.

It is time to take a dream and make it come true. You no longer desert your own longings by harnessing yourself to anybody else who looks like they may have a good idea. Instead, you focus your intelligence on discovering which avenues are right for you.

Wind Creating comes to love long periods of isolation, and finds too many demands upon her become claustrophobic. Her ideal partners and friends are very individual characters with a high degree of self reliance and independence. In this unrestrictive company she is a witty, entertaining and intelligent presence.

Wind Resolving

Wind Resolving is a mature man, deep in thought at the window of the solitary retreat of a windmill. This person is able to use the enquiring, scientific mind to serve and conserve the planet rather than adding to the Earth's distress.

This person is likely to be somewhat reclusive and reserved. He has little or no small talk and on initial acquaintance may be difficult to engage in conversation. However, if you find out what his passion is, a very different and inspiring individual will emerge.

Wind Resolving may represent someone who is a mentor figure for you. He evokes deep respect through his dedicated contribution towards alleviating present-day plagues and problems. He does not seek to foster this sense of awe and may be bashful in the presence of demonstrations of affection, appreciation and acknowledgement. His ambition is to assist those who choose to be his students to look beyond the known and carefully charted avenues of academic development.

You will find, on close acquaintance, Wind Resolving is capable of a tremendous depth of love. You must meet with him out of your own fullness and with your own developed sense of purpose. If he seeks a partner, he looks for someone who is not threatened by individuality and who does not resent his passionate devotion to his quest.

AN OVERVIEW

of the Hearth Songs

The Hearth Songs are the forty cards traditionally known as the Minor Arcana. The Hearth Songs reflect everyday joys, disruptions and self deceptions. They highlight the ways in which we respond, often unseen or unnoticed by others, to the small conflicts and challenges occurring in daily life.

It is easiest to learn the individual meanings of these cards by first seeing the patterns which run through the Hearth Songs. Before reading further, you may find it helpful to lay out these forty cards in front of you, placing them in numerical and elemental order. Jot down the immediate impressions you have.

The Hearth Songs represent four elemental energies: earth, fire, water and air (Earth, Flame, Wave and Wind Songs).

All Earth Songs relate to the physical world. When they appear in a reading they pertain to the practicalities of living in a physical body on Earth today. Earth Songs are relevant to such issues as health, financial situations and possibilities, home life and the actual environment in which you live, and the changes you want to make in these areas. These cards reveal your relationship with giving and receiving. Also portrayed is your desire to be in the world or your choice to withdraw from external input for a time.

Flame Songs all in some way address your creativity, sources of inspiration and the manner in which you live out your chosen spiritual path. Also depicted is your response to people who challenge your stance on issues about which you feel passionate. The Flame Songs show whether your gifts and talents are being used in a focused manner or whether you are dissipating your potential through lack of commitment and direction.

Wave Songs explore feelings in all forms: love, hate, despair, disillusionment, friendship and the zest for life. They portray the qualities present in all your relationships. Wave Songs can assist in clarifying further action, either to heal and enhance empathy and communication, or to withdraw and reassess in order to avoid further pain and misunderstanding.

Wind Songs characterise the ways in which you use your intelligence — or don't use it, as the case may be. Most of us are aware of the mind's potential to be used either as a creative power or as a destructive force. Wind Songs depict these polarities and make it clear when negative thinking is undermining tremendous creativity and joy. The imagery of the Wind Songs reminds us that changing our thought patterns will dramatically change our ability to deal with and to resolve conflicts and complex issues. Tapping into the right brain — the world of meditation, visualisation and intuitive leaps — is portrayed, encouraging us to find new and creative alternatives to solving contentious issues.

Each of the four elemental suits of the Hearth Songs has ten numbered cards. Here, a little knowledge of numerology will further your interpretations.

All First Songs, traditionally known as Aces, represent new beginnings and the rush of energy, enthusiasm and initial commitment accompanying this fresh start. First Songs may also signify a gift, as life sends goodness and well-being your way. A more specific interpretation will depend on the suit.

A comparison of the First Songs in order will give a clear picture of the subtle differences in interpretation within each suit.

The First Earth Song offers some new and secure footing on the physical plane, which will give you the courage to take a risk and to see how far you can leap.

The First Flame Song sees the emergence of tremendous passion for a new project, through which you can simultaneously express your values and ideals. Often these plans involve others, who are swept along in the heat of the moment.

The First Wave Song is the gift of love and healing and the restoration of harmony. You are able to nurture yourself; a heightened sensitivity towards your own needs is drawing fulfilment into your life.

The First Wind Song signifies a flood of new ideas. Your mind hungers for a challenge. This may well be a time of beginning a new period of concentrated study and training which will ultimately open up many more options for you.

Twos represent the desire for balance and harmony. However, because the new has disturbed the old pattern, adjustment to change is essential. Life will feel like a juggling act until you have assimilated the new paradigm.

And just when you think all's going smoothly, along comes Three — often an unexpected complication which may be confusing, or add an illuminating new dimension. Threes become an initial testing time. Explore the unsettled feeling or situation further. It's important to allow new developments to emerge in order to avoid becoming trapped in a rut created through fear of the unknown.

Fours depict the need for structure, planning and stability. Limit setting and personal safety may be important issues for you now. It is time to become clear about the boundaries required for your plan or project to evolve. However, if you become uptight about changes and decision making, this tension will result in rigidity. You may be holding on too tight. Keep those hands free enough to reach out. Sit quietly until you hear the inner voice giving direction.

Fives show how you deal with conflict and also encourage you to courageously look at the root of those disturbances. Fives remind you to trust your instincts and to use or gain skills in communication and negotiation. Remain open to solutions you may not have seen as possible.

Sixes assure you you're on the right track, even if you've had to change your path in order to attain a sense of rightness about your life's direction. Sixes are indicative of your developing confidence, self esteem and ability to enjoy your successes, sharing your gains with others.

Sevens assure you that patience and continuing commitment is valid, even though you may not yet see the fruits of your labours. At times life has a 'plod, plod, plod, am I really getting anywhere?' feel to it. Hang in there — a new burst of energy is coming. It's important not to become too dreamy or make sneaky short cuts, otherwise you'll end up losing ground and ultimately making a lot more work for yourself.

Eights are decision-making times. Anything can happen — it's up to you. It's vital to remain conscious of the central issues and outcomes you want, otherwise you may become distracted or despondent and give up on something which, with continued time and input, will flourish. However, it is also appropriate to look at what you're investing your time, money, emotions and creativity in. Reappraisal and withdrawal may be necessary. Becoming too agitated will be counter-productive, however, causing delay and stagnation.

Nines are end points — for better or worse. You see the results of your actions. If you have been true to yourself, you will have a tremendous sense of inner well-being and your outer life will reflect this. If you haven't succeeded as you'd hoped, don't spend too much time in self recrimination and in mulling over the past. New beginnings are available to you. If you are able to see your experiences as your teachers, you will use your insights to turn around destructive patterns and make a break from repetitive cycles of despair.

Tens take this energy of completion one step further, to something greater than you anticipated. You will either

realise there are many more steps you can travel or else you
will recognise that some significant changes in perspective
are necessary. You may want to seek guidance to find ways
of consciously resolving conflicts and dilemmas.

The First Earth Song

The First Earth Song portrays a mother breastfeeding her baby.
Together they inhabit an invisible yet palpable cocoon, spun
with nourishment, protection and love. This is a primal
experience of intimacy and security.

This image signifies wholeheartedly giving yourself to your
purpose, and feeling, as a consequence, the rhythm of life is
flowing through you and singing in your heart. You have the
wondrous experience of feeling your interrelatedness with all
beings and elemental forces. You recognise at a profound level
your vulnerability and dependence upon Earth as mother and
provider.

Life is blessing you now, showering goodness upon you. You
have the exhilarating sense of being in touch with what you
really want to do. No matter the outward manifestation of your
purpose — to dig a garden, to conceive a child, to begin a new
career, to move into a new creative phase — your doing is
arising out of your innermost being and you feel you are
making the right choice.

The First Earth Song also reminds you that your physical
body — a vessel simultaneously functional and sacred — may
be your greatest teacher. Always remember to listen to and be
guided by the sensations and subtle messages your body is
giving to you each moment.

The Second Earth Song

The Second Earth Song depicts a woman sitting on a fence, almost clinging to it as she avoids making a decision.

You may be experiencing discontent in your current circumstances. New and attractive opportunities present themselves and you are uncertain which way to leap. Often this image signifies a time when you feel stymied, working hard and making slow progress. You may be unsure about your motives for wanting change. Do you really need a total change, or just a new perspective? In this state of vascillation you may hope events will lead you in a certain direction, without your having to make a definite choice. By withholding too long from making a move, the impetus wanes and inertia takes over.

To align yourself with your dream you will need to move out to the edges of your definition of safety and security. Saying yes to one option can mean saying no to another, and this is not always a comfortable process.

Is your life is cluttered with trivial expectations and commitments which you could let go of to make more space in your days? Have you burdened yourself by taking on responsibilities which could have been delegated? Are you maintaining patterns to please and placate people in your life? By consciously facing the compromises you are making, you will also face your fears. It is easiest to bring about transformation in your life when you recognise the trepidation which holds you back.

The Third Earth Song

The apprentice sets his sights on his goal, which is, as yet, far away.

This is the time to imprint the vision of your desired destiny in your creative mind, so that you will be continuously drawn to this point, even though on a day-to-day basis you may sometimes lose focus, direction and purpose.

The apprentice has fresh enthusiasm and has not yet experienced any setbacks. He carries with him his tools and all the knowledge he has gleaned, which may come in handy somewhere along the way. The key at the centre of the maze opens the gate to the Magician's sacred garden.

The Third Earth Song portrays the effort you are making to find work and physical circumstances which are deeply satisfying, where you have a sense of contributing towards the creation of a more harmonious world and, at the same time, receiving back the benefits of living in tune with your talents.

Find people who will offer some direction through the maze. Look for study courses and training opportunities which will allow you to achieve the skills and proficiency you desire. Reject ideas which weigh you down, preventing you from making a start. It is all too easy to decide you are too young, too old, too poorly educated, the wrong sex. There will always be justifications luring you away from taking a new initiative.

Put yourself in the company of people who are enthusiastic about learning and who will encourage the persistent effort needed to fuel you through any disappointing and difficult experiences.

Cast doubts aside and begin!

The Fourth Earth Song

The Fourth Earth Song has a whimsical quality, softening the constrained, isolated and perhaps fearful experience portrayed in the card. The image denotes a time of organising, prioritising and making secure your material world. You may be budgeting and saving for future goals in a disciplined manner.

Your focus appears to have become narrowed: all work and no play makes Jack a dull boy! Events around you evoke mistrust and timidity, causing you to lock yourself away. Retreating in this manner somehow disempowers and diminishes you. The person slumped at the desk is worn out with the current state of affairs. The books may be balancing, but the rest of his life isn't.

The piggy bank makes a bold bid for freedom, cheekily waving farewell as it heads off through the open cat door. (A way out will always present itself, if you look for it.) The piggy bank is, for many people, a memory from childhood, when savings were delighted in and eventually used to purchase treasures which brought so much pleasure. The piggy bank represents the forgotten concept of happiness which escapes you in your earnest quest. You have neglected your personal riches — warmth, love, humour, generosity, compassion and good company — in the effort to get ahead. This fortune is not elicited through financial gain which has been achieved to the detriment of your health and peace of mind.

Use the power money has to bring pleasure and satisfaction to your world and to the people who share your life, otherwise your wallet will be full and your heart will be empty. Also assess whether your availability to loved ones is of more value than the financial gains made during your long absences from them.

The Fifth Earth Song

Time is speeding up to the degree whereby you feel you are under intense pressure. Gone is the deep, soothing, rhythmical tick-tock of the grandfather clock from childhood nursery rhymes. Instead, alarm bells sound in your head and you don't seem to be able to turn them off. There are never enough hours in the day or appointment slots in your diary to fit everything and everybody in. The second hand becomes a treadmill to which your feet have adhered. The days are merry-go-rounds of ceaseless activity.

How you are managing to keep going? What is the price you are paying? How is your physical body coping under the strain? Is the relentless pace affecting your sleep and invading your dreams with disturbing images? Illness may be a manifestation of the stress you are experiencing, alerting you to the need to slow down and reassess your priorities.

The Fifth Earth Song is an image of imbalance. Ancient timekeeping flowed with the movements of the stars, moon and sun and thus continued to connect people with elemental, diurnal, tidal and seasonal patterns. This connection is now, for the most part, severed. City dwellers in particular are ruled by rush hours, public transport schedules, time sheets, sirens, whistles, hooters, intercoms and pagers.

Time has become a tyrant, with many people seeing the only choices as either slavish obedience or outright rebellion. The former particularly occurs when you like to be seen by colleagues as a diligent and indefatigable worker. The rebellious behaviour of perpetual lateness and breaking appointments is an unfair and ineffective method of trying to regain some control.

Make a list of all the pressures which make inroads on your time. Reflect on the degree to which each item weighs you down and write down exactly why you feel burdened. See if you can regulate any aspect of each circumstance — you will find there are few situations in which you have no control at all.

Place the Chariot image beside the Fifth Earth Song. Contemplate all the ways in which you could steer an easier course for yourself. Regularly remind yourself, 'I'm doing the best I can in this moment, and sometimes near enough is good enough.'

The Sixth Earth Song

At last everything is coming together and slotting into place in what seems to be a perfectly preordained pattern. A greater picture is revealed, leading you to feel balanced and appreciative of the ample sufficiency which permeates all aspects of your material world.

The Sixth Earth Song signifies the culmination of successful negotiations, the finalising of a significant purchase, or a career move which rewards training and study. Where other parties are involved in bargaining, everyone plays an equal part and, through this power sharing, is satisfied with the outcome.

The camel, partially in view, represents a certain stubborn tenacity of character. You have the strength to survive in arid conditions by drawing on inner reserves. You are a real survivor when you need to be.

The rugged work shoes depict your willingness to do much of the hard ground-work to establish yourself in your chosen venture. The red boots stand for your cheerful persistence, wading through the mud and boggy patches and keeping your goal in sight. The flippers indicate that you take regular time out from the many pressures which tend to escalate as a project is finalising. A good blast of fresh air and sunshine will help free up your lateral thinking.

The fences, keeping the goat from the vegetables, relate to the use of boundaries which aid, enhance and make secure your endeavours. Sense what is required for your circumstances. For example, legal structure and guidance from an accountant may be valid safeguards. The fences and gates also alert you to be mindful of respecting other people's demarcation lines, such as religious and cultural protocols and taboos.

Your efforts have closed the chasm between your dreams and your reality.

The Seventh Earth Song

The Seventh Earth Song is a pregnant pause. You are fully in tune with inhabiting a physical body, flowing with your inner rhythms and cycles. You also live in harmony with seasonal changes, understanding the timespan involved in growth and change. You recognise the situations which cannot be hurried; if forced, the outcome will be a less than whole version of the dreams you nurture.

You have done all you can for now — a little bit of weeding here and there may be required, but no more than this. Appreciate the growth you have set in motion, which will come to fruition. Trust this waiting time. Let go of hankering for completion.

Enjoy every stage of creative manifestation; recognise and willingly do all the mundane and painstaking work required to bring forth the exquisite fruits of your labour. Feel the seasons alive in you. What is being born in you? What is dying within you? What is being reborn in you? Find ways to fully connect with the seasons and moon cycles. Allow yourself to merge with the feeling of being part of a greater pattern.

The patience portrayed here is not a passive waiting. Rather, it is a wide-awake, alert attentiveness, relaxed yet ready for action when the impetus comes. The clarity you have in this phase will evolve into a fine perception of what the next appropriate transition will be.

The Eighth Earth Song

The Eighth Earth Song is a joyous celebration. You reap the rewards and satisfaction of having established yourself in the workplace, in a way which is challenging and satisfying. You are fully fledged and flying! You are receiving acknowledgement and acclaim for your consistently high standard of work and for your professional ease and artistry.

The Eighth Earth Song may well herald a time of transforming your hobby into work which provides a viable income. Thus, your work and your pleasure combine. It may be appropriate to explore some aspect of teaching your skills. You will perhaps find it more financially viable to create a joint business venture with colleagues, rather than setting up on your own.

The house in this image symbolises your opening all the doors within you, allowing hidden and diverse talents to emerge and become realised. Too often, one aspect of personal achievement dominates, stifling what could be very rewarding pastimes.

Before you go to sleep, ask your dreams to show you which door to open to lead you to greater fulfilment.

Draw a picture of a house, with the rooms each representing aspects of your physical life. Feel what sort of house you are. Draw rooms which portray your health, your work (paid and unpaid), your hobbies, your dreaming place and your responsibilities. Create rooms which symbolise your friendships and your loving, nurturing qualities. Feel which rooms you would like to change and which rooms contain your undeveloped potential. Are there any rooms which frighten you? Depict whatever lurks in the room, causing you to pull back from entering.

Now choose one room that you would like to begin transforming, bringing more colour and balance into your life.

The Ninth Earth Song

The Ninth Earth Song is an image of wholeness. This card signifies that you are undergoing a series of transforming events which are showing you the connections between the physical plane and the spiritual plane. You may appear detached and separate from your usual circle of family and friends, as this self containment often helps to crystallise your thinking.

The star at the centre of the image represents the light of the love you have come to give expression to in this lifetime. The woman and child together reflect the blend of fresh innocence and maturity, which gives the ability to see the humour and magic which is present and yet often unnoticed in so much of ordinary life.

The circle encapsulating these two figures symbolises an aura of sacred protection in which the experience of healing intensifies. You may use meditation and rituals, or perhaps physically retreat to some place which nourishes and restores you. Find whatever boundaries best serve you.

The bed of pansies signifies the appreciation of the fantastic designs in nature. Delight in each new breath, in being touched by sunlight and brushed by the wind.

The vulnerability which arises when you acknowledge and appreciate the fragility of life also opens you to a deepening of wordless contemplation.

The Tenth Earth Song

The Tenth Earth Song depicts a pair of performers receiving accolades and appreciation following a brilliant and seemingly effortless performance. This image symbolises outward, laudatory acknowledgment of your perseverance and commitment, which has led you to excel in your chosen field. This is the culmination of months, perhaps years, of preparatory work.

Allow yourself to bask in the pleasure your success brings. You know that more dedicated work lies ahead of you. In this moment, however, relax and let yourself take in the significance of this milestone. Just as you once had mentors who challenged and inspired you, now you in turn accept this role, willing to share your skill, knowledge and expertise.

The stage here serves as a symbolic reminder. Fully embrace your current life choice and remember you are more than any roles you play. Wear your costumes loosely enough that you can step out and beyond them without attachment.

Perhaps, when looking at this image, you identify more with the members of the audience than with the performers. This is also a delightful and often uplifting experience, imbibing the passionate and glorious talent which washes over you. However, you may need to ask yourself whether you would like to enjoy a bit of the limelight. Perhaps you have supported and encouraged someone else in their dreams and now it's your turn to find where you shine.

The First Flame Song

The First Flame Song signifies the ripening of a creative process which has gestated within you. You have nourished and strengthened this dreamchild and now you are in the birth throes and the potential which has lived within you becomes visible.

The lotus opening around the baby's crowning head signifies a powerful transition, which may be perceived as a mystical initiation.

An awareness of death is often present as a natural counterpoint to birth. In aligning yourself with whatever you most desire, you may need to give up activities, habits and relationships which sap and dilute your sense of purpose. Give voice to any grief and fears which arise. This will help you to move through the passage of personal evolution more easily.

There comes a time when, in order for expansion and flowering to occur, you must move out beyond secure and comfortable confines. The First Flame Song says you have reached the limits of growth in your current niche.

When the First Flame Song appears in a tarot spread, it is one of the strongest images indicating the conception of an actual child.

The Second Flame Song

The Second Flame Song is the synthesis of the logical mind and the intuitive mind, of linear thought and creative inspiration, of the scientist and the mystic.

The image of the woman and man, both gazing into the night sky, is a harmonious one. These two are seeing and marvelling, each in their own unique way. They remain in comfortable proximity while immersed in their experiences. Their shared reflections will create a greater affinity between them as they see through each other's eyes, as well as their own, the magic of the unknown beyond the known.

Just as astronomy and astrology were originally unified, so there exist ancient alliances beneath superficial dichotomies.

The Second Flame Song urges you to approach your options with openness. If your mind is very stuck in believing you have to make divisive either/or choices, you may benefit from hearing other people's points of view. This gives the opportunity to take a broader view before you make your decision.

The Third Flame Song

The Third Flame Song encourages you to to juggle the opportunities available to you. The three women here represent different facets of the same person. This is the fun stage of experimenting by acting out the variety of roles which appeal to you.

The eggs which are the focus of this play represent the beginning of the search to find out which path is for you. All the eggs are whole and unblemished. This is a joyful time full of untested enthusiasms. Eventually, to progress further, you will need to crack open your dreams and see if they do contain fertile possibilities.

Now is the time to keep lots of doors open, with a wait-and-see attitude. Don't let your desperation to achieve a sense of purpose govern you. It's important not to narrow down your options until you've taken a good look at all the diversity life holds for you.

The Third Flame Song often indicates a physical move of some sort is needed. By broadening your horizons you are more likely to find a niche which seems to be specially marked out for you.

The Fourth Flame Song

The Fourth Flame Song reflects the importance of understanding and flowing with the rhythms of your body. You may need to let go of destructive habits which keep your body artificially hyped up. Give yourself enough rest and relaxation, so that you can feel your natural energy levels waxing and waning. In this way you will avoid bouts of frantic activity followed by collapse.

This image portrays Woman tuning in to the cycles which will flow through her body from life to death. Recognise the powerful influences of inhabiting a vessel which is in a constant process of transformation: the changes of puberty, the choices and challenges surrounding fertility (or infertility), the physical changes which come with bloodwane and growing older.

Cradle and protect yourself. Feel the ebb and flow of power and vulnerability, of giving and receiving, expanding and contracting, of expressing and withholding.

Use your body as your teacher and let it become your dearest friend. Take pleasure in coming home to yourself.

The Fifth Flame Song

The Dreamer comes to you as a reminder to recall and take heed of the messages which come to you in your sleep and those which flit unannounced through your daytime awareness. These subtle communications often come in pictures and sensations rather than in verbal pronouncements, so you need to be able to listen through all your senses.

The Fifth Flame Song signifies some disruption and discord around you. You need to respond in a highly intuitive manner to the circumstances which you fear could engulf you. The owl protects. This bird of the night signifies your ability to see your way through confusing and shadowy times by remaining alert and observant.

The strong shifts and upheavals depicted in the earthquake, the tidal wave and the eruption denote a time of unearthing and revealing the source points of the crises which rock your world.

The dreaming woman retains a watchful awareness in the eye of the storm and the hours of darkness and she comes through these turbulent experiences wiser and stronger.

The Sixth Flame Song

The Sixth Flame Song portrays the dancer, bringing to life the powerful rhythms which have always lived within her, longing for expression.

Dance is often used in sacred work as a way of journeying back inside the self. Surrendering to the movements which seek release in your body, you break through entrenched patterns and emotions which have moulded your physical form.

Everything comes pouring through when the dancer moves beyond all the rules and structures, and finds the pulsations which have throbbed faintly within. True sensuality and passion have no preordained technique. The mind lets go and the body leads. When you are able to maintain conscious focus and move with wild ecstasy, you shake free everything which keeps you feeling stifled and limited. By dancing out your pain, joy, anger and fear, you unclutter yourself and create a space for bliss to expand in you.

In this ecstatic experience you meet with the reflection of your own divinity, as you dissolve and merge with the rhythms of the life force.

The Seventh Flame Song

The Great Escape!

For too long you have felt powerless in your circumstances, as if the controls of your life are in the hands of some faceless martinet. Your security has also become your misery and in your conformity you have forgotten how to dance.

Suddenly you have a crystal-like vision of how trapped you are. In recognising this you also clear the way to break free. Often only one or two decisive actions are needed to set in motion a chain reaction which will release you. This flush of freedom brings fresh perspectives.

The Seventh Flame Song heralds a change in viewpoint. No matter how much anybody else has guided and supported you, the actual act of breaking free is one you must do for yourself. Courage is a key ingredient here. If following your heart means facing the possible disapproval of powerful and significant people in your life, then this is the risk you may need to take. Look long and enquiringly at your life. Ensure your choices are made from a place of strong self respect and understanding. Then cut your losses and take a leap!

The Eighth Flame Song

The Eighth Flame Song portrays a maypole dance. This ancient ritual from the northern hemisphere is traditionally a spring celebration and symbolises the reawakening of dormant energies. Any lethargy is shaken from the body with movement and dance.

You are ready now to see the patterns behind the seemingly random events which chaotically enter and exit your life. With this knowledge it is possible to create harmony between your outer world and your inner sense of spirituality.

Imagine you have eight trees which you keep neatly in tubs and tend to regularly. Eventually in their small pots they will reach their growth limits and even begin to die. Transplant the trees to terrain which suits each, and wait and trust. The earth will continue her mysteries and a far greater flourishing will occur.

The time is ripe to commit yourself either to one particular project, or to just a few which you can explore fully and actively. Share your reflections. Encourage others to take on any ideas you cannot follow through; allow friends to reap from the seeds you sow. You don't have to do it all yourself. If you try to hold on to everything, you will become frustrated.

The blossoming magnolia tree here symbolises the flowering which is possible with rain, sun, patience and a little help from your friends.

The Ninth Flame Song

Exhilaration and tremendous personal satisfaction are the themes of this image. The overflowing yolk indicates you have found the source of your creativity and you are able to manifest a multitude of expressions from this place. The egg cracking open also reveals the new life and vitality you bring to all you do.

This person launches into expressive endeavours, not held back by the absence of degrees and diplomas and extensive training.

The Ninth Flame Song is often the revisiting of a passion from your childhood — painting, dancing, singing, drama, music. You may choose to rediscover your delight in a long-forgotten pastime. It's a fortuitous time for you to pursue lucrative ways to turn a hobby into work you love to do, so hunt for this opening.

Cracking open your own creative desires means taking a risk. Whenever you reach for your dreams, all the fears of failure, ridicule and doubt come rushing at you; it is far safer to imitate than to step into your own visions. It is not only your own misgivings which hinder your progress. People who have chosen security to the detriment of their creativity have no hesitation in warning you of the improbability of living out your dreams.

Through knowing this apprehension does arise, you will be able to recognise it and not be deterred from your purpose.

The Tenth Flame Song

The Tenth Flame Song is a time of evaluating and questioning, when the bright sparks of passionate inspiration have died down and seem to be rapidly cooling embers. What is often needed now is someone who can guide your thoughts and reflections — someone who has enough distance to discern the overall themes and patterns and help you to find a pathway through the maze.

The tarot spread is like a photo album, clearly depicting the interplay of attitudes and choices you are facing. A tarot layout can also create some boundaries for your confusion. Each image may express a different vantage point from which you may view your circumstances. This helps you move out of a limited vision of the alternatives open to you. The cards also bring to light the inner characters who tend to run the show of your life, and they reveal the hopefuls who lurk in the wings longing for a bit of the limelight.

The exquisite stained-glass window gives a feeling of a sanctuary where you can safely reveal your vulnerability and uncertainty, knowing you will be met with support and respect.

The First Wave Song

The last remnants of the storm retreat. This is the light at the end of the tunnel and the opportunity for a new beginning. The rainbow here symbolises the joy and positive changes shining from you right now. Some shift in your perceptions and circumstances leads you to feel whole and wholesome. The raindrop is a tear born of ecstasy. The experiences of separation and isolation vanish and are replaced by a sense of coming home.

These feelings of bliss arise when you experience uncond-itional love. In this state of heightened sensitivity, you experience yourself as being a part of some greater purpose or plan and the edges of your ego-identified personality soften.

The lotus pattern hints of the possibilities for transformation which are brought into full view in the Lovers card. The First Wave Song is a great falling in love and may be beyond a one-to-one meeting. You may feel very drawn to a particular community, or to a piece of land, or to a spiritual teacher. You may have a vision of some action which you feel moved to make in response to being so deeply touched.

The Second Wave Song

This exuberant image of cherubs playing on the crest of the fountain is a celebration of new love. You see the highest and the best in each other, and a certain innocence and open vulnerability surrounds your union. Memories of previous loves and disappointments vanish and, with them, any lingering cynicism and disenchantment.

The buoyant cherubs portray the lightness with which you bounce through the days when new love comes your way. This sensuous romping brings a sparkle to your eyes, a glow to your cheeks and the fragrance of happiness envelops you.

The Second Wave Song gives rise to feelings of having met your soul mate, leading you to describe the other in superlatives.

The cherubs are, for the moment, blissfully unaware of the ocean behind them. The deep waters represent the journeying into the depths of each other, as well as the heights. This is, as yet, an untested love and much about each of you remains undivulged. Enjoy the light and have courage, when the time comes, to face the shadows together.

The Third Wave Song

The Third Wave Song depicts the joy of friendship, which carries with it the ease of familiarity and longevity. These three know each other's strengths and weaknesses, and together they complement and support each other. 'Together, we make one genius!' is the refrain of this trio.

The maturity of the love here has moved beyond the struggles and miseries of the proverbial eternal triangle. The triangle is also the symbol of the visionary. In this atmosphere of hilarity and relaxation, each expresses her dreams and desires.

The bathtub, in the form of a cauldron, signifies the ripeness for transforming these dreams into creative ventures. The bubbles are like fleeting crystal balls in which are glimpsed future possibilities.

The Third Wave Song is a time for group projects, mutual encouragement, and the sharing of talents. Choose people who are cooperative rather than competitive. Let your unique qualities blend together without allowing any one to become swamped and submerged.

The Fourth Wave Song

Frogs into princes — or is it princes into frogs? The fairytales don't seem to be coming true for you and everything has a vacillating and mutable quality.

The Fourth Wave Song depicts a period of confusion and disappointment. This often occurs when you have placed some beloved on a pedestal, from which they inevitably must fall. The learning here is to move beyond casting the people in your life into roles of heroes and villains, saviours and saboteurs.

This image also relates to periods of rapid metamorphosis in your own life. You may have a transforming experience which leaves you feeling at one with the pantheon of gods. Then, moments later, you find yourself brought low, cursing at an inconsiderate driver or cheerlessly drenched in a downpour without your umbrella.

The stepping stones at the prince's feet remind you to keep practising balance, even if it seems to virtually elude you. This card is an encouragement to love yourself, warts and all.

The Fifth Wave Song

The Fifth Wave Song is an experience of broken dreams and lost opportunities. It is a time of self recrimination and doubt, of mulling over the past and becoming quite lost in wishing you had acted or chosen differently.

It is important to take the opportunity to acknowledge and grieve your loss. However, it is also vital for you to recognise when your sadness is diminishing, so that the sorrow does not become a habit and an excuse to escape facing the future. If you summon up your courage and change your focus of attention, you will immediately see how much that you had forgotten or ignored is waiting for you.

This image of the butler also calls for you to create balance between serving others and taking care of yourself. If the former is to the detriment of the latter for a prolonged period, a culminating crisis will alert you to the urgent need to take your own feelings and needs into account.

Allow healing to be drawn into your life now, as avoiding this will only lead to stagnation and unnecessary pain.

The Sixth Wave Song

The Sixth Wave Song, depicting an old waterwheel, symbolises the presence of or the yearning for contact with a dear and trusted friend.

The flowing water represents freshness being brought into your current relationship. Whether you can make physical contact or whether you are separated by land and water, reach out now and send your love.

The circular motion of the wheel indicates a certain constancy — a friendship which has stood the test of time. The wheel also denotes the practical nature of this familiarity, using the power of the lovingness which is generated to serve each other through the ever-changing seasons and circumstances of your lives. Your actions demonstrate to each other your mutual cherishing and appreciation.

The mill house, hinting of stored grain, further highlights the nourishing and sustaining nature of this friendship.

The Seventh Wave Song

The water lapping at the edge of the bank becomes a soothing lullaby and the warmth of the late afternoon sun is a soporific. In this drowsy space, between waking and sleeping, a reverie unfolds. The fishing line symbolises the desire to access the subconscious. The bulging fishing net contains the dreams and desires which have been drawn out of hidden depths and into view.

This is a time when you are aware of a multitude of possibilities, tantalising choices and the burgeoning of creative ideas. The difference between the rod and the net depicts the significant disparity between your knowing what you want and actually summoning up the wherewithal to reach for these treasured goals.

In the absence of decisiveness this cache of fertile imaginings will slip beneath the surface and vanish. If you can find within you the strength to pick up a pen and jot down your thoughts, this will create a thread which will lead you back to your dreams more easily.

It is very tempting to remain in this experience of suspended reality, particularly if there are difficult decisions to be made in your life. Allow this floaty slumbering to relax you and to give you an expanded view of your options. Then bring yourself back from this fantasy world and do something constructive to merge aspirations with action.

The Eighth Wave Song

The Eighth Wave Song is a melancholy image of separation where you had longed for union. This image is often characteristic of a situation in which you recognise you no longer fit. Perhaps you never fitted, but nevertheless tried to force yourself. You feel there is no place for you in this structure anymore. Although you continue to have heart attachments to these people or circumstances, you know you must go.

You have a sense of loss in breaking away and also the understanding that the experience of loss will ultimately be greater through not moving on. Doubt and anxiety may have preceded your decision, as your choice may have distanced you from family, colleagues or acquaintances. Feelings of sorrow and perhaps regret may mingle with love and beautiful memories. This image heralds a turning point in your life which you know has been coming for some time.

The Eighth Wave Song at times also indicates restless discontent and blame. It is a self-defeating pattern to be able to see every possible cause for your misery, except your own part in creating angst in your life.

Are you continually moving on — from jobs, from love affairs, from countries — always hoping happiness will find you in some new place? If this aspect of the image rings true for you, recognise that this emptiness can only be completely filled when you come home fully into yourself.

The Ninth Wave Song

It's time for celebration! Good will and good humour are overflowing and everyone joins in the party. Let loose and don't keep yourself serious and separate, whether the cause for jubilation is yours or someone else's. If it is your joy you are celebrating, allow it to froth up and bubble over so that you magnify the feeling of delight as you share your happiness.

This may be the cathartic release following an intense rite of passage; it is needed to express the heights and depths to which you have been moved. The Ninth Wave Song also signifies a community of like-minded people who have pulled together, achieving a long strived-for goal.

Laughter has its own sacredness and healing and now is the time for its magic to touch you.

The Tenth Wave Song

An abundant sense of love and harmony creates a protective sanctuary in which new birth occurs. The swans form a heart-shaped avenue, here symbolising the passage of transformation which is opening to you through the strength of love in your life.

This birth or rebirth may take many different forms and may manifest physically, spiritually and creatively. The silver and gold eggs resting on the lily pads speak of a union which has allowed each of you to glimpse the jewel within yourself and your beloved. Love brings to life the potential which has always lived within you.

This discovery and sense of imminent awakening has the feeling of an evolving and refining of your purpose and destiny. The alchemy created by this deep, mutable and abiding love flows over to touch the lives of many.

The First Wind Song

Like the resonating gong, inspiration vibrates within you. The sun on the horizon of the new day heralds the moment of conception of a new idea. Your mind is wide open, like a conduit drawing in the multitudes of possibilities. The First Wind Song is the very beginning of a creative process — a whirlpool of potential into which you unhesitatingly allow yourself to be drawn.

This is a time when you have an expanded and heightened sense your life purpose and capabilities. You may see the unfolding of an entire project in vivid detail, and desired outcomes will be seen with intense clarity. Here, for a brief time, you know and trust a full cycle of events before even beginning to set any actions in motion.

The First Wind Song can blow through you like a current of ecstasy. The challenge is to harness the ideas and dreams before they dissipate. Otherwise, this gift of foresight dissolves, and you sidestep the opportunity to draw some real magic into your life.

The Second Wind Song

The two gulls wheeling in a clear sky signify a peaceful and somewhat solitary time. If you choose to be with people, you will be with those few dear friends with whom you can be alongside in comforting and companionable silence.

In this atmosphere of support which needs no words to affirm its presence, you have time to examine the whole terrain of your life. With calm and objective compassion you rise above the isolated hills and valleys of your experience. In this place of expanded vision you calmly formulate plans. The Second Wind Song indicates a time of integrating your reasoning and logic with your senses, hunches and subtle perceptions.

Outwardly it will appear that not a lot is happening, and you may be perturbed by the amount of daydreaming you are indulging in. However, the whirlwind of the First Wind Song becomes a gentle breeze and you need time to decide how you wish to draw this vision into your life.

You discuss the ideas you are formulating with people who can toss ideas around lightly. You want to reflect on all the possible avenues before committing yourself to any particular action. Also, your thoughts may seem too insubstantial and fragile at this stage, and may crumple under harsh scrutiny. Let your visions float a little longer.

The Third Wind Song

Here three people are locked into a situation which will not end in reconciliation and mutual understanding unless a whole new approach is used. As well as being split off from each other, they are each projecting aggressive thoughts and emotions which are veneers protecting feelings of vulnerability and woundedness.

All Threes disturb the balance and initial security found in Twos. Threes are the risk involved in growth, change and expansion.

The Third Wind Song depicts an upheaval in which each person fights to win; everyone will end up losing unless someone recognises the foolishness in the drama. If you can, let yourself disengage from the ever more tangled explanations and amplifications and just have a good laugh or cry. You need to tap into a feeling mode which will help you arrive at the heart of the matter.

The Third Wind Song portrays these three as equal parties and is a reminder to you not to adopt a position of either righteous indignation or victimisation. If you can see your own contribution to this turmoil, you may be well on the way to recognising and unravelling patterns of ineffective communication. Thus, the conscious examining of a painful interaction can act as a catalyst for change.

The Fourth Wind Song

The longing suddenly arises within you to get away from it all. The Fourth Wind Song signifies a sense of urgency surrounding your need to vanish to somewhere offering peace and quiet, where no one can possibly reach you and make demands upon you. This image is a playful fantasy of great escapes: the splendid isolation of outer space or a perch on top of a lunar mountain; maybe a celestial ship will swoop down and carry you away from your present responsibilities.

You realise you have become too caught in the rigid and oppressive structure of schedules and routines and need a break. This may mean cancelling previously made plans and opting for time alone. Although you may fear you are letting people down, your overriding need is for time alone.

The Fourth Wind Song calls for active withdrawal. You may plan to go away to an isolated place, where it is very difficult for the concerns of your daily life to reach you. However, this idea may be a response to exhaustion, and it may be enough to hide out at home.

Whatever you choose, you require a time of mental relaxation to allow you to feel you are the creative author and director of your own life story. Use the space you have created to revitalise yourself — listen to inspiring music, read books which fuel your imagination, gaze into the enormity of the night sky and surrender yourself to a belief in your potential, beyond the limitations of fear and self criticism.

The Fifth Wind Song

The eye of the storm has passed and you are reeling in the aftermath, feeling buffeted and bedraggled. Some disturbance has swept through your life. Even if you were only observing from the sidelines, you have not escaped undercurrents which have caused you to falter.

This image often signifies realisations which strip away illusions; you are left with stark reality. You perhaps have been carrying mental padding around certain people or certain situations. You may have had some investment in seeing through the softening contours of this padding.

Now any cushioning is gone. Your life changes as you recognise relationships and experiences which you can no longer sustain. You look at your life with crystal-clear vision, amazed that you've been settling for smudgy focus as a safe option to keep friendships, businesses or contacts going. You realise how much mental effort it has taken trying to keep it all together. Now everything has fallen apart — yet there is, through all the disjointedness, a sense of peacefulness and relief.

This is a turning point for you which will require some break with the past. See the new sun rising. Daylight comes, showing all which remains to be dealt with very clearly.

The Sixth Wind Song

You feel as though you have been under a tremendous amount of pressure. You may feel you have totally lost the connection with the inspirational vision you held in the First Wind Song. Myriad setbacks, complications and unanticipated obstacles all seem to crowd in to block your path. You may have moments of paralysing self doubt which almost squeeze out of you the impetus to carry on towards your goal.

However, the geese in this image assure you this season of despair is changing. Your instincts and inner wisdom have not deserted you — if you are able to focus on trust, rather than on fear, you will rise above the turmoil of the mind.

You know something of the past has irrevocably changed and you are ready to move on, yet the future is not clear. The mind panics and believes it is confused. Sometimes you need to find the courage to move away from circumstances before you are shown the direction in which your life will open up.

This is a time to surrender to the gentle winds of change which are nudging and tugging at you.

The Seventh Wind Song

Here is a mysterious image which seems to tell a story of misdirected reproach. The bold magpie clasps a shiny treasure in his beak and is, unwittingly, the catalyst for the child's misery. Perhaps the child has made up stories before and artlessly fabricated the truth. Now he withdraws, shamed and disbelieved.

Trickery and confusion abound. In the nest the young cuckoo hatches first, a greedy imposter who will toss out all the newer, smaller and more vulnerable chicks. All around you, as a child, you may have observed people constantly ducking and wheedling their way out of telling the truth, convincing themselves they have valid reasons for making this compromise.

Now, as an adult, you may continue these often subtle patterns of deceit or misrepresentation, as you may believe honesty doesn't pay. However, this approach has a perpetuating quality. By using these tactics you will pass this way again: situations you try to glide around rise repeatedly to meet you until you are no longer able to sidestep them.

Use this time to look within and find words to clarify exactly what is happening. This will not be a comfortable time for you, but pussy-footing around the issue no longer rests easily with you either. If you act now, you will prevent the snowballing effect of evasion and half truths building up and possibly rolling on top of you.

This image may, alternatively, signify circumstances in which you are being ostracised for saying what you think and feel. So often gossip is condoned, and a direct and frank approach of speaking about grievances is frowned upon. It is time to retreat to the cave of the High Priestess, or to the edge of the Hermit's pool, until clarity and resolve come to you in the healing, silent wisdom.

The Eighth Wind Song

The Eighth Wind Song speaks of a time of losing your sense of being connected to the greater whole. This feeling is not necessarily brought about by change in external circumstances. You are unable to recognise within yourself the unique treasure you are.

The woman believes she stands on the edge of a precipice, but does she? Fear is the scarf which blows across her face, preventing her from seeing and naming the abyss in her life. Perhaps this path of unhappiness is well known to her, for it appears to be a well-sealed and maintained route. Sometimes some gentle self examination is needed to ascertain whether you find it easier to endure despondency than risk the possible discomforts of exploring a new and unknown terrain.

At times this image may signify actual abuse within a person's life; self esteem and resources may have been whittled away to almost nothing. Yet the woman folds her arms around herself in a gesture of protection and preservation. The bird gliding towards her has been sent on the air currents to help her find a way out, above and beyond all the weighty limitations. This bird may come in the form of a friend, a therapist, a lawyer, a healer — someone who will act as a guide for her.

The Ninth Wind Song

The mournful bird sings a song of sorrow and loss which is tinged with self pity and resentment. Perhaps she once sang happily in what seemed to be a gilded cage. Whatever the previous circumstances, she now perceives herself to be in a remote and isolated place; the craggy escarpment offers no place of shelter. The gnarled tree here represents the tenacity of spirit which will survive, no matter the circumstances. Survival is one thing, though, and growing fruitfully is quite another.

The cage is not the barred prison it may initially seem. There is an opening here offering a way to freedom. Past defeats may have left you feeling listless and resigned to your present circumstances.

The glow of the sun warms the bird's wing-tips. This image signifies the growing recognition of the need to turn towards positive and sustaining experiences which will in turn generate more lightness and joy. The still stretch of water beneath the bird symbolises the need for a gap — a period of emotional calm. This is also an important time to reflect, without self recrimination, on the events which have led you to this place.

The hills and valleys of future experiences lie beyond the water. Take the time now to fully understand and resolve this passage of your life. Re-evaluation now will lead you to more hospitable landscapes.

The Tenth Wind Song

The Tenth Wind Song represents the revisiting of a situation or relationship which has previously lured and entangled you. It is an image of incompatibility, not of evil intent. The spider is just doing what spiders do, weaving a web to catch its food. This is a reminder to observe the web from afar and not to challenge the inevitable.

Whenever you come into close proximity with whatever has become the root of your misery, you experience an addictive fascination with being drawn in, despite your better judgment. You can so easily seduce yourself into waving aside your firm resolve to steer clear of this path.

Sometimes when you have recovered from a crisis point, you may feel the need to return and face the person or the addiction to prove to yourself you can now handle the experience to your advantage. This justification for renewing contact needs to be accompanied by a clear vision of what you hope to achieve. The opportunity is here to illuminate and transform a previously damaging experience.

This image offers you freedom from this cycle of injurious attraction. By bringing the light of conscious understanding to shine on this self-defeating pattern, you will be able to free yourself in a way you never thought possible. It is often people who have broken out of an addictive cycle who are able to guide others through the tricky territory with compassion and tremendous insight.

PART FIVE

THE MYTHS
BEHIND THE MIRRORS

S ymbolmaking and storytelling go hand in hand. In creating *Songs for the Journey Home*, sometimes the image came first and the fuller understanding of the picture evolved as Dwariko and I reflected on the nature of the archetype. This was the case with the image of the Star. At other times events and stories came first, giving rise to an image which encompassed the qualities of the experience. In particular, Beyond Judgment and the Ninth Earth Song exemplify this process. The following stories are the myths behind the mirrors.

The Star Woman

There is a beautiful Star Child, named Soft Radiance, who lives happily in an abundantly twinkling constellation, full of stars who love and cherish her. Her favourite pastime is to watch Earth and all the chaos, beauty and hectic goings-on. She is fascinated. Most of all, she is intrigued by the behaviour of human beings, who seem to create so many problems for themselves, in what looks like a wonderful playground. She often daydreams, 'If I were a human being I would . . .'

One day, she asks her Star Grandmother to tell her about humans — and the story astonishes Soft Radiance. Star Grandmother explains that all the people on Earth were once Stars — bright, luminous, with amazing vision and knowledge. Despite this, they had longed for a romp on Earth. They were always full of the conviction that they would take all their wisdom and farsightedness with them.

Star Grandmother explains that it is rather complex living in the human body and, even with the best intentions, it takes enormous awareness to remember you are a Star.

'Soft Radiance, it is a strange and magical thing to be human, for although the human looks like a single entity, each of these beings is made up of five elements: earth, fire, water, air and spirit. This spirit is the remembering — the Great Remembering you are a Star.

'And,' Star Grandmother continues, 'the elements can remind you or cause you to forget. It is a fine juggling act, and most humans create great strife while they practise the juggling. Too much fire totally consumes — with greed, with rage, with hatred. Too much water drowns you in torrential emotions, pulling like a whirlpool. Too much earth means you have your nose so close to the ground working you never glimpse the beauty around you — and, although you achieve much, it never brings joy. And too much air means you only trust what is seen with your eyes; too much arguing, discussing, proving and debating means that all words become empty.

'Then, there is Spirit — Great Remembering. Even here is turmoil, as the world is full of beliefs, all trying to disguise themselves as Great Remembering, all saying, "You will remember if you follow this path."

'However, the absolute wonder of humanness is when all the elements are balanced and Great Remembering occurs, because then you become a Star again, living on Earth in a human body and helping with the work of Great Remembering. When the time on earth is complete, if you have remembered, you will become a Star in the Great Constellation again. If you forget, you continue coming back in a body of five elements until you remember your true essence.'

Soft Radiance is enthralled by this story, and asks, 'How do you know so much about this human life?'

Star Grandmother replies, 'Because I made the journey myself, of course, and now I have returned.'

Soft Radiance gazes down at Earth, feeling herself drawn to this little planet. She becomes very watchful, noticing in the midst of the turmoil there are Star lights, scattered over Earth, which twinkle back at the Stars in the constellations. Soft Radiance is now determined to go to Earth — and determined she will not forget who she is.

So, one night, a glorious shooting star is seen in the night sky, just as a child is being born, and thus Soft Radiance begins her earthly journey.

Earth is incredible; so incredible Soft Radiance totally forgets she is a Star. And so she lives and dies many times. Each life is a juggling act and, sure enough, it is as Star Grandmother said it would be: passions, tragedies, loves, friendships, wars, enemies, cruelty, torture, and very occasionally a tiny moment of balance.

After each life finishes, there is a period of darkness. In the darkness is just one night when Soft Radiance becomes a Star again. For this happens to all humans — they are given, through death, one night of remembering. As the lifetimes go by, Soft Radiance has inklings of her true Star nature, which become stronger and stronger with each successive life.

So we come to her present lifetime. During her Star night,

before this incarnation, she has said again and again, 'I *will* remember!' This remains as an echo within her. As a child in the stillness of the night, she hears, 'Remember, remember.' This frightens her, and she runs to her parents' bed and hides between them. Despite the fear, she feels a strong pull within her to explore the spirit.

In this lifetime there is a reasonable balance of earth, fire, water and air. She lives in a beautiful country and has loving parents, enough to eat, clothes to wear and work she loves. There is enough balance amongst these four to explore the fifth — the spirit. This becomes her juggling act and a turmoil in itself. She sees a glimpse of Remembering in many earthly doctrines, but there are also dark clouds blocking the light.

She has many dear friends and lovers who are in the process of Remembering. There is a lot of forgetting too — lots of imbalance. Soft Radiance begins to be able to see the Star glow in herself and in others. Even when there is Great Imbalance, she sees the lights dimly shining through. In fact, sometimes Great Imbalance seems to be the way through to Remembering.

Soft Radiance begins caring for people who are in Great Imbalance. She seems to be able to draw out the Star light even in these situations of Great Imbalance. She begins to see these times as opportunities for Remembering — even Small Remembering. Just as the fire is going out, as the water is running dry, as the earth is cracking and the air is feeble, the Star light shines through.

This amazes and also exhausts her. It is very tiring to be around Great Imbalance, and so exquisite to be present at Small Rememberings. Sometimes, there is only Great Imbalance and she feels she too is burning or drowning or crumbling or struggling for breath.

Her Star Grandmother is right, though: there are Stars on Earth who have attained Great Remembering and these people come into her life when she needs help. Soft Radiance recognises Great Remembering in the Star person and sees flashes of it in herself.

At times, she becomes overwhelmed and miserable. 'How can I possibly become a Star when I am so imbalanced?' she wails. More and more frequently, though, she finds ways to achieve balance, and sees how to help others with Remembering. She realises it is not enough to worship the Star light in another — she has to remember it herself.

And Remembering becomes like a gentle discipline, a drawing back from the huge engulfing swings of Great Excess.

As this story is being told, Soft Radiance is Remembering more than Forgetting, and there is more Balance than Great Excess. She is able to recognise Star light in its multitude of manifestations.

Now Soft Radiance can hear Star Grandmother speaking to her and knows this is a true and trusted voice of her beloved ancestor, who has known, forgotten, then reknown the Great Mystery — of being a Star, a Sleeping Star and a Reawakened Star.

The Bird and the Anchor

The image of Beyond Judgment evolved out of a myth I wrote and a series of drawings I did over a period of about seven months in 1991–92. I had felt the need for the objective understanding and reflective listening of someone outside of my circle of family and friends. I was blessed in finding the degree of integrity I was wanting in two women therapists who work in the field of transpersonal psychology.

A period of regular individual sessions and several workshops enabled me to make peace with my broken path with Bhagwan Shree Rajneesh, the spiritual master whose teachings have profoundly influenced my life.

I retell the myth here as I first wrote it. I envisage that, by its metaphorical nature, it is transferable as a story of the insight and the restoration of self determination which comes by facing losses which have left us in some way wounded.

During an individual session I had a very strong image of myself as a bird with an anchor around my ankle. I recognised the bird to be the expansive, intuitive, trusting self which is surrendered to life to guide me. The anchor represents all the hard spiritual lessons I learnt when I lost my trust in Bhagwan's vision. And so the story begins . . .

There is a bird who lives on an island, and has done so for five years. The bird is ready to fly again, but only with trepidation. The bird is afraid to fly high because it has flown so high before and crashed so hard.

The bird is reluctant to leave the anchor, which is too heavy to fly with, but is a reminder. And the bird is terrified that, in the joys of flying, it will forget what it has learnt and crash — and that this time it will die. But it is time to return to a home glimpsed briefly in times of total relaxation and gentleness, and the only way there is to fly. To fly is to risk crashing, yet not to fly is never to reach home.

So the bird takes a piece of shell in its beak, fashions it into the shape of an anchor and threads seaweed through it to become a necklace.

One morning, just as the moon is setting and the sun is rising, the bird farewells the heavy anchor, which is made for ships not birds. The bird has been in the company of the anchor for so long that it is like farewelling a safe and trusted friend. But a bird belongs in the air and an anchor belongs on the ocean floor. And the bird has its amulet; it can fly with its little anchor and therefore will never forget the night of the shipwreck and the loss of the captain, the crew, the vessel. All broken, all drowned, all lost — save the bird and the anchor. The bird had flown with that ship for so long, and had loved the wind in the sails, the storms, the safe harbours and the bounty of fish in her wake.

Years have passed. The bird has seen other ships in the distance and yet she has stayed with the anchor. Now it is time to go. It is such a beautiful morning — so still, so glorious — and the bird rises into the air, very hesitatingly at first. The bird circles around and around the anchor, imprinting the image forever in its mind.

The bird speaks in the keening calling way of birds and says, 'My beloved anchor, you were all I had left when our ship was washed up, and I have clung to you, as if held by invisible threads of fishing line. For years I have never dared to fly far from you. You have been my only tangible memento and I thank you for staying up here on the beach with me. But see, you are all dry and rusty, and I know you long to live at the bottom of the ocean in your true resting place.'

The bird flies to some nearby islands to test its wings, and stays there for a few weeks. The bird can fly back and see the anchor and talk to the anchor.

One day, the anchor says to the bird, 'Little bird, the season is changing and it is time for you to go. Tonight there will be a storm, and the ocean, which is my true home, will reclaim me. And I will become beautiful. I will become the home for coral and crabs and fish will swim by me and octopuses will rest on me. And I will lose my brittle contours and my memories will become gentler.

'You and I, little bird, have talked so often of why the ship hit the reef — both of us so angry for different reasons. My job, as the anchor, was to keep the ship safe, but I failed and was too afraid to let you fly off again.'

The bird replies, 'And I failed because I didn't see the reef ahead — even with my vision, I didn't see it coming.'

As the bird wheels above the anchor, the anchor speaks and says, 'Whenever you need words for safety you will be able to talk to me. Just rest on the ocean and I will hear you and send you my thoughts. And you will tell me of your wonderful flights — of all you see, of all you meet. Your journeys will make me mellow and my thoughts will keep you safe.'

The storm comes and takes the anchor to the sea floor. The bird flies above the storm and watches the splendid fury and the power of the waves.

Whenever the bird comes to a new place, it traces an anchor in the sand with its beak and watches the incoming tide reclaim it. And, forever, the bird remembers those years when the bird wouldn't fly and the anchor wouldn't sink. The memory of the shipwreck becomes like the far-reaching beams of a lighthouse, allowing the bird to navigate through storms without crashing.

The bird flies on, with the shell anchor around its neck, and shows other wounded birds how it could be safe for them to take flight again.

Valerie's Story

The Ninth Earth Song is dedicated to Valerie, a wise woman and visionary whom I had the great privilege of sitting with, learning from and caring for in the final eighteen months of her physical life, which ended in March 1992.

One evening I was sitting on Valerie's bed, marvelling at the exquisite velvety texture of the petals of a bunch of pansies picked from her garden. Their delicate and transitory perfection was almost painfully beautiful. Valerie told me this story of a recent experience with her little grandson, Jacob, while they were at her home.

'I was going down the steps very slowly, because I was having trouble with my breathing. Jacob was following me out into the garden, which was ablaze with flowers. Suddenly, I was aware of him coming to a standstill behind me, and then he gasped, "Grandma, Grandma, they're all looking at us!" And I saw through his eyes this sea of pansies, all with their faces upturned to greet us. And then, as if perfectly timed by some cosmic cue, a gentle breeze came up, and the awe in his voice intensifed. "Look, Grandma, they're dancing!" '

Valerie described to me the receptivity and sensitivity which was opening in her. Through being unable to rush or push herself towards goals, her appreciation of momentary jewels magnified. To see God through her grandson's perceptions brought her so much joy. She increasingly came to value simplicity and had little patience for the complex and tangled webs she saw people weaving around themselves and their relationships.

Valerie was truly a wounded healer, a teacher who generously shared with those who wanted to listen her journey and the lessons she was sent daily. She was never content to soften the experience by clinging to beliefs. She allowed everything she held dear to come up for review and, in this surrender, we whose lives touched hers were blessed.

Tarot archetypes release their messages and mysteries to us when we take the time to reflect on the ways we experience these symbols in our own lives. Creative visualisation through guided imagery can be a very powerful experience, assisting us in creating this link between our personal experiences and their symbolic representations. The process of creating symbolic links allows us to acknowledge the significance of life events we may previously have labelled mundane and insignificant.

The following three visualisations offer pathways into discovering our own symbols and simultaneously gaining greater insights into several tarot images. These three visualisations, as with the entirety of *Songs for the Journey Home*, emphasise the concept of wholeness as an experience of balance, where all aspects of ourselves are greeted and honoured. This approach is profoundly different from the quest for perfection which requires the judging and discarding of those aspects of ourselves we deem flawed and therefore unacceptable.

Thus, in the visualisation process, allow all the images that flicker on the periphery of your inner vision to reveal themselves. It is important not to judge images as good or bad but, rather, to wait until they tell their own stories. Often we receive symbolic images which may reveal their relevance to us weeks after we first envisage them.

These visualisations are designed to be read slowly, in a safe and tranquil setting, free from disruptions. One person needs to read the visualisation to the other participants. If you are alone, read the transcript onto an audio tape, and then replay it so you may enter fully into the experience. Make sure you are warm and comfortable before you begin. Often it is best to be sitting up rather than lying down, because of the tendency to fall asleep. Have paper, a pen and coloured pencils beside you so you can make notes at the end of the visualisation.

It is important to allow space for the symbols which come to you to float around in your awareness for a day or two. It may be appropriate to have a gap of a few days before entering into another visualisation.

Begin and enjoy!

Spirit Bridges — Meeting with the Luminary

The following visualisation is a meeting with the Luminary, the Wise One who exists as an archetype within the psyche. It is important to make regular contact with this guardian, recognising this as a powerfully knowing aspect of yourself. It is all too easy to be dazzled by the brilliance of a charismatic and convincing teacher and to forget that, ultimately, you alone can best realise the most appropriate ways in which to express your truth, love and creativity.

Place the image of the Luminary in front of you. You are now ready to begin.

Sit comfortably — settle into the body. Feel the breath washing in and out — in . . . bringing freshness . . . and out . . . effortlessly shifting any disturbances. Now, with each in-breath, feel you are drawing a pillar of light through the crown of your head and right through the body in a cone of light . . . Keep drawing the cone of light with each in-breath . . . and now . . . with each out-breath, feel the soft darkness of earth flowing through you from your feet upwards . . . in . . . light . . . out . . . darkness . . . balancing day and night . . . outer and inner . . . receiving and giving . . .

And in this state of balance, you now surround yourself with a beautiful bubble of protection — shimmering — a sanctuary — see the colour and breathe in its radiant luminosity. Feel this aura around you creating a secure boundary . . . in front of you . . . behind you . . . under and over you . . . a permeable film . . . allowing only positive influences to penetrate, at your invitation.

Breathe deeply now . . . feeling the replenishing qualities of this refuge . . . a safe place . . . to relax . . . to pause . . . to listen . . . to sense . . .

You become aware of a deepening receptivity . . . a waiting . . . you feel the approach of a totally loving and trustworthy Being who has taken on a physical form to meet with you. You hear the rustle as this Being of light approaches your sanctuary . . . gently . . . towards you . . . through your translucent shield, you allow your eyes to be met . . . receive the love which pours through this Being . . . beholding you with love . . .

Choose now, if you will, to expand your sacred space, inviting this guest to slip through the boundary to meet with you.

In this Being's hands is a small, flat, silk-wrapped gift. You know this gift is yours and that this is the right time for you to receive this gift.

This Being speaks no words aloud, but the loving voice resonates within you, 'Now is the time to recognise your wisdom — to honour the lessons and experiences which life has brought to you thus far — to recognise that this is a significant lifetime, in which the possibility for transformation is ever present.'

Breathe deeply now . . . relax in safety . . . Unwrapping the silk now — the exquisitely woven silk — you reveal three cards, all face down, each with the same glorious pattern on the back.

The voice of your visitor sounds gently within you with these words . . .

'These cards will reflect to you symbols of your knowing. When you turn the first card over, be willing to meet with . . . to recognise . . . the symbol for your truth . . . your truth, whatever this may be . . . reach out now and turn the first card over . . . breathe deeply now . . . allow the image to strengthen in its form . . . acknowledge yourself . . . your truth . . . this is a reflection of your inner knowing . . . breathe in this image . . . this symbol of your truth . . . consciously accept the understanding of truth which is deep within you.

'This recognition of truth is a guide for you . . . the light of your intuitive knowing of truth . . . to hold up as a light for your path . . . to show the true way for your feet to walk.'

Breathe deeply now . . . feel the wisdom of this truth alive within you . . .

'Now focus on the second card, and as you reach out to turn it over, be willing to meet with . . . and to recognise . . . the symbol for your love . . . the source . . . deeper than sentiment

. . . deeper than attachment . . . turn the card over, and allow the symbol for your love to strengthen in its form . . . acknowledge this reflection of your lovingness . . . consciously accept now this understanding of love which is deep within you.

'This recognition of love is a guide for you, available to you whenever you choose to tune in to your intuitive knowing of love . . . use this symbol as a light for your path . . . guiding you to people and experiences which will recreate this inner knowing of love in your outer world . . . so the inner and outer become more constant . . . harmonised . . .'

Breathe deeply now . . . feel the wisdom of this love alive within you . . .

'Now focus on the third card, and as you reach out to turn it over, be willing to meet with . . . and to recognise . . . the symbol for your creativity . . . for when we are true to our path . . . and when we manifest love in our lives . . . creativity arises . . . turn the card over . . . allow the symbol of your creativity to strengthen in its form . . . acknowledge this reflection of your creativity . . . consciously accept this understanding of the creative power within you, available to you whenever you choose to tap into this source of true expression of the self.

'This recognition of creativity is a guide for you . . . your symbol is a light for your path . . . leading you towards manifesting your life's purpose, in this body, in this lifetime.'

Breathe deeply now . . . feel the wisdom of creativity, alive within you . . .

See before you now your three symbols on the cards — truth — love — creativity. Breathe in these images — for they are yours — reflections of your deep, knowing wisdom.

Breathe deeply, and with each breath, the symbols on the cards fade, as their essence — their fragrance — enters you — taking this understanding deep inside you with each breath.

You are aware now of this Being, signing to you a blessing . . . having awakened the Wise One within you . . . now leaves you alone . . . alone and full . . . able to bring this knowlege you have recognised out into your life . . .

In a moment I am going to count from five to one, drawing you back into the physical world around you, and you will bring your symbols with you . . .

Five . . . being aware again of your protective cocoon . . .

Four . . . breathing in this colour . . . so it washes through you . . .

Three . . . with each breath, the outer boundaries of your sanctuary unravel, drawn inside you . . . carried on your in-breath . . .

Two . . . becoming aware of the space around you . . .

One . . . opening your eyes now, feeling refreshed and replenished.

At the completion of this visualisation, take the time to write about your protective bubble, recalling its colour and texture. Describe the Wise One. Draw the symbols you received on the three cards, jotting down your impressions about these images and the guidance they currently give you. Personal symbols are very powerful, often offering far more wisdom and guidance than we initially see. It is helpful to keep your drawings in a place where you will see them regularly, so they continue to tell you their stories — your stories.

The Scales — Balancing Dualities

Justice is often experienced as the quest for equilibrium. The following visualisation focuses on balancing inner polarities of light and darkness, stillness and movement. Lay the Justice card in front of you and begin . . .

Close your eyes now . . . settle into the body. Feel your breath washing in and out . . . bringing freshness and effortlessly shifting any disturbances.

Now, on the in-breath, feel you are drawing a pillar of light through the crown of your head . . . sparkling, crystal-clear light — it may feel like a waterfall of clarity being poured through you. Know this light as your intelligence . . . the lucid precision of your mind . . . serving you . . . guiding you. And now allow this light to take form and become an image . . . an image of your active intelligence . . . how you can use your mind for your highest good . . . to support you in your life.

Breathe deeply now . . . knowing you will remember the sensation, and your image for intelligent clarity, let this vision fade . . . as you become more focused on your out-breath . . . feeling the soft darkness of Earth flowing through you from your feet upwards . . . you sense your whole belly as a cave, a warm . . . moist . . . dark . . . shadowy cave . . . full of the treasures of your intuitive knowing . . . a place where you can rely far more on sound and touch . . . smell and taste . . . to find your way . . . for you know, from this wise place, that things are not always what they appear to be through sight alone. And now, allow these shadows to take form, and become an image . . . your own image of your intuitive knowing . . . recognise how you can use this knowledge for your protection . . . for your nourishment and direction finding.

Breathe deeply now . . . knowing you will retain the essence . . . the fragrance of this cavern of wisdom, let this image fade . . . as you become focused now on your arms and hands . . .

gently open your hands out, palms facing upwards . . . like scales in balance.

And bring your attention to your left hand, and envisage the sun setting just behind your fingertips — see the glorious interweaving of light and shadow . . . the magical playtime of day and night . . . until day relinquishes to night . . . and become aware, in your own life, of the things which are at your fingertips . . . or which are slipping beyond your grasp . . . in this time of sunset, be aware of skills, of qualities you are letting slip away . . . which you would like to draw back . . . to have the pleasure of using . . . and recognise those aspects of your life which are outmoded, which you want to release yourself from.

Allow the colours of this twilight time to merge and take form, becoming an image of whatever needs to be let go of, or reborn . . . acknowledging this wise part of youself, which recognises the right time for freeing you up for transformation.

Now feel the sun dip down, over the horizon of your left hand — darkness . . . night . . . dreaming time . . . Become aware of your right hand . . . the rising sun now, gleaming through your fingertips . . . new day . . . new beginnings . . . new opportunities . . . the old gone . . . the new arriving . . . fiery, active, decisive, determined . . . any doubts and fears realised in the dark of night are vanquished . . . here is purposeful movement forward . . . a path found . . . a way made clear. As you gaze into the brightness of the rising sun, see an image which expresses the harnessing of your abilities to achieve your goals.

Breathe deeply now . . . and with each breath, feel yourself drawing these four energies — of crystal light and shadowy sensing . . . of the sun — dying and being reborn in an endless cycle . . . drawing these energies into your heart and solar plexus . . . and feeling your out-breath creating a whirlpool, mixing everything together . . . all aspects of yourself . . . in-breath . . . drawing . . . out-breath blending . . . until the whirlpool stills . . . gradually . . . becoming a tranquil pool . . . Look in at your reflection . . . the reflection of the essence of yourself . . . allow the image to intensify . . . becoming a symbol which contains the qualities you sense in the reflection you see.

You hear the sound of running water, and the pool becomes a stream, rippling, dancing, flowing, bubbling. Recognise the part of you which will not let stagnation occur . . . the Wise One who knows when you have rested enough and it's time for movement . . . ripples . . . creating waves . . . rapids . . . sense the aspects of your life which are alerting you to the need for change and growth.

As you listen to the stream's song and laughter, sense the balance of the clear pool and the cascading stream . . . the balance of the rising and setting sun . . . the balance of conscious clarity and subconscious whisperings. Embrace this fullness of yourself.

And now, breathing fully and deeply, returning to the room around you . . . gently opening your eyes . . . softly focusing . . . fully present here.

After completing this visualisation, you may like to draw a picture of your body, and the various symbols, colours and energy fields you experienced. Even if you don't yet fully understand the meaning behind the images, record them now, and through reflection their significance will eventually be made clear to you. The visualisation can often highlight some practical course of action necessary to achieve a greater degree of equilibrium.

The Tree of Woman Spirit

This visualisation is the synthesis of the lessons, gifts and wisdom brought to us by the High Priestess and the Empress. We also experience the elemental qualities of earth, fire, water and air which are found throughout the tarot. Lay the images of the High Priestess and the Empress in front of you and begin . . .

Sit comfortably — settle into the body. Feel the breath washing in and out — in — bringing freshness, and out — effortlessly shifting any disturbances — a most natural, balancing rhythm — which brings you into a sense of alignment with your true nature.

Allow the ebb and flow of your breath to take you deep within yourself — sinking . . . sinking . . . below all the details and dramas which tug for your attention. Let them be . . . without any effort . . . just let the breath take you beneath them.

Only the sound and flow of your breath holds your attention, easing you into a deep sense of relaxation. And from this place of relaxation, imagine yourself in a beautiful retreat house . . . at dawn. You arrived the night before and have slept deeply. Gradually, the new day enters your dreaming. Sunlight touches you . . . you hear the birds in the nearby bush calling . . . the roar of the ocean mingles with the fresh breeze — carrying it's salty tang to you.

You feel a strong sense of being drawn outside . . . and you rise from your bed and dress. Picking up a small rucksack, you step out, into the early morning. Across the field, you see the beginnings of a path through the bush . . . and the sound of the ocean comes from beyond the trees.

You feel the wet grasses against your legs as you make your way towards the path. The bush is exquisitely inviting — dappled light dances . . . hear the sounds . . . see all the shades of green . . . smell the dampness — all alive.

Feel your feet on the path — the care you take over roots and wind-blown trees which cross your way. These are not obstacles — they give you a sense of dancing along . . . constantly adjusting your pace to allow yourself to absorb and become a part of all the beauty around you.

As you round the next twist in the path, your eyes are dazzled by the brilliance of the rising sun. Moving forward into the light, you see before you the silhouette of a huge, ancient tree, in the middle of a grassy glade. You are aware of a potent quality emanating from this tree . . . She is the Tree of Woman Spirit. Come as close to the tree as feels right for you . . . amongst the thick, gnarled roots which stretch out, embracing Earth before disappearing beneath her surface.

You perceive the nourishment and strength channelled from the roots, through the trunk, and out to the newest foliage. You begin to feel waves of this nourishment and strength being given to you also.

This tree is not only a place of shelter . . . she offers sustenance for you. Listen to the Tree of Woman Spirit . . . She will teach you to recognise the places to spread your roots . . . the hidden sources of vitality which will allow you to weather storms and droughts. You make your way slowly around the base of the tree now . . . towards the sunlight . . . and you see a beautiful cove before you . . . the ocean glistening in the dawn light. Standing amongst the outstretched roots . . . a feeling of expectancy arising within you.

Ripples appear on the water and a woman surfaces and stands before you. You recognise this is Wave Woman, queen of the realms of feelings, emotions, generosity of the heart and discernment in love. See her come towards you . . . you move forward to greet her, walking from the rough roots, through the grass to the soft sand.

You can see deep into her eyes now. She reaches out towards you . . . and in her hand is a gift she has brought especially for you. Smiling, she hands it to you. This gift is a symbol of the message she wants you to carry. You recognise the gift and sense its meaning, breathing in the truth and protection it gives you.

Looking into her eyes, you send your heartfelt thanks to her . . . and she turns — and dives beneath a wave.

Breathe deeply now. Knowing you are to keep this treasure with you, you put it carefully into your rucksack.

You wander down one end of this little inlet . . . towards the caves tucked into the side of the hill. As you approach the caves, you see the figure of a woman emerging out of the damp darkness. You pause and watch as she approaches you.

You know this is Earth Woman, queen of all manifestations of earthly life . . . she who knows all the ways to bring the practicalities of life into balance with the spirit.

See the basket she carries on her arm. She is close enough now for you to look into her eyes. She reaches into her basket now and draws out a gift for you . . . she hands it to you. Breathing deeply now, you sense the loving purpose of this gift, and the message it holds for you. You send her your thanks as you look into her eyes . . . and she now turns and walks back to her grotto in the hillside.

Gazing again at your gift from Earth Woman, you then place this in your pack, together with your gift from Wave Woman.

You move slowly to the opposite end of the beach, gathering driftwood as you go. You realise you are to make a fire. You find the perfect place. After laying the wood, you take matches from your pack and light the fire.

Watching the rising sun . . . listening to the crackling of the dry wood . . . looking into the haze of the flames . . . relaxing deeply . . . breathing deeply . . . in a soft trance . . . you see a figure dancing in the flames. Whirling and swirling . . . alight yet never burning . . . all glittering scarves . . . and all tinkling bracelets.

Allow your eyes to meet her shining eyes. See the sparkle of her pearly teeth as she laughs and smiles. You know this is Flame Woman — woman who knows how to live passionately — who transforms her inspirational dreams into realities. She weaves her creativity into everything she touches. She now playfully removes one of her decorations and tosses it to you. She spins faster and faster, and you feel her heat — her intensity — and now . . . she is gone.

The gift she has left you is warm in your hands . . . see it now . . . this symbol of the message she wants you to carry with you.

Breathe deeply now. Rest in your understanding. Placing your gift in your pack, you carefully pour sand on the fire to put it out.

You make your way back to the massive tree — the Woman Spirit Tree.

You hear now the rustle of wind . . . the beat of a bird's wings . . . hear its cry. Looking up, into the brightness of the day, you see a bird circling overhead and you realise a woman is sitting firmly on its back.

The air is full of the rushing, throbbing sound of the bird's wings.

You recognise this is Wind Woman — she who knows the mysteries of the mind — who has a farsighted vision which she flies towards, using intelligence and, at times, isolation to focus her purpose.

You see now this Bird Woman is holding something in her hands . . . a gift for you . . . which comes sailing through the air. Reach out and catch it . . . it is for you.

See now what she has given you . . . recognise the message she brings to you.

Breathe deeply now as you meet her eyes . . . The bird wheels and flies up . . . up . . . gone.

You go now and sit amongst the roots of the Woman Spirit Tree . . . gazing softly at the ocean, the caves, the fireplace and at the empty sky.

You open your pack and lay out each of your gifts . . . feeling the strength, wisdom and guidance which have been given to you.

Know that deeper and deeper understandings will come to you . . . this is only the beginning.

Feel again the waves of nourishment coursing through your body . . . recognising these gifts as tangible reminders of the intangible treasures you carry within you.

You close your inner eyes — knowing your surroundings are gently dissolving in the now bright, bright light of day.

And, in a moment, you will hear my voice counting from five to one, bringing you back into the present experience of your life.

Five . . . becoming aware of the space and the sounds around you . . .

Four . . . knowing you bring the wisdom of these gifts with you . . .

Three . . . coming up from the depths of your self knowledge . . .

Two . . . bringing with you the restoring qualities from this retreat . . .

One . . . opening your eyes now, feeling refreshed and replenished.

After completing this visualisation, take time to write about this experience, and to reflect further on the nature of the path, the tree, the beach, the qualities of the four women and the gifts you were given. Drawing these symbols may also heighten your understanding of the messages they bring to you, to help you in your current circumstances. You may like to collect together items which represent these gifts, and place them together on a small altar, to honour and give thanks for your journey.

TUNING IN

Some Ideas on Tarot Reading

Here are some practicalities for those of you who are
wanting 'how tos' for reading tarot for yourself or for
another person. See if these ideas work for you and also
discover your own ways. When the suggestions relate to
reading for another person, I refer to this person as the
friend. This is because, in my experience, tarot is most
commonly used as a vehicle for intimate sharing with
someone you know well. Although I name one person as the
reader, a tarot reading is a focal point for an exchange
between two people and both participants are free to
contribute their insights. The cards provide a framework to
the dialogue and assist in releasing the intuition and
creative intelligence of both the people who are looking at
the cards.

I find it vital never to rush a tarot reading. For a full
reading such as the Celtic Cross layout, I like to allow at least
an hour and up to an hour and a half — though no longer
than this. I set a limit, as the mind can begin striving to
grasp at more and more straws, rather than absorbing the
answers revealed thus far. The mind, which loves to toss
around problems, may create a resistance in the person to

beginning the implementation of changes which will restore harmony.

I always like to read in privacy with the friend, unless the reading is specifically regarding the others present to an equal extent. However, I usually find it most effective to read for people individually before a joint reading. Having thus elicited the concerns of each person, I am able to help them to move more rapidly to a mutual understanding.

I generally only look ahead to the direction for the next six months or year as, once underlying disturbances are recognised, significant changes are inevitable.

Rituals of some kind are often a part of tarot readings. They may be used to create a gap between being caught up in worldly issues and entering into a greater degree of sensitivity and silence. Rituals are like spring-cleaning the link between the logical mind and the creative intelligence.

I prefer very simple preparations — a clean, clear environment and a smooth wooden tabletop, if possible. I may light incense. I do not usually have music playing as I find it distracting. I do like the friend to sit by my side, so we are facing the cards together. I sit the person to the left of me because I find the left side of my body is more sensitive to perceiving the subtle vibrational qualities of the other person.

When I am reading for someone new, I like to know of any past experiences with tarot. Many people continue to associate tarot with black magic and therefore the desire for a reading may be tinged with fear, which reduces the ability to recognise their own truth reflected in the cards. I make it clear I am not a fortune teller, and that, as I see it, the purpose for using the images is to explore issues, finding underlying obstacles which are keeping the person from a sense of fullness and joy.

I give a general overview of the cards, describing the nature of the Life Songs, Shell Songs and Hearth Songs so the friend has an understanding of the form tarot takes. This introduction also serves to relax and orientate us both, creating in each of us receptivity for self listening.

Before beginning the reading, we discuss questions the

friend wants to ask. Depending on the trust and openness the friend feels, the true concerns may or may not initially be mentioned. I begin with one question the person may be comfortable with. As we move into the reading, anything of significant relevance will find its way in.

Tarot does not generally lend itself to rigid yes or no answers. The layout becomes like a photo album — the cards are the snapshots of whatever events and issues surround our enquiry. Hence, when we see the overall picture symbolically represented before us, right directions reveal themselves. However, we have total freedom to choose whether or not to alter course. It is not for the tarot reader to demand any adherence to the pathway revealed in the tarot layout.

Life itself will bring us the same inner lessons — merely altering the outer form — so we are brought to face essentially the same situations, over and over, until we reach a resolution and move on. We are all at many different levels of resolving the same lessons about truth, love, life, death and power.

I move on to shuffle the cards until they feel alive with the warmth of my hands. I then ask the friend to shuffle the cards, and at the same time to focus on the issues surrounding the question which is being asked. A deep, relaxed breathing pattern can also assist in contacting the various feelings associated with the question.

The following is an effective and simple spread I frequently use.

Shores and Bridges

The first step in this layout focuses on the shore on which the person currently stands, in relation to their question. Once the friend has shuffled the cards, I arrange them face down in a fan, with each card accessible.

I then ask the friend to choose three to six cards which represent where she is right now, in relation to the situation she is asking about. For example, 'What am I currently experiencing in my workplace that causes me to feel dissatisfied?'

Choosing cards is not to be a laborious time of indecisiveness, otherwise the reading will, in all likelihood, reflect the fears and indecisions of the mind, rather than the person's inner sense of rightness.

Some people choose by floating their hand above each card, sensing the right ones. Others gently touch the cards, back and forth. Some choose by softly gazing at the cards, feeling behind their eyes which cards to reach for.

These first three to six cards will expand and clarify the question. This allows for the perceived problem to be fully aired, rather than remaining a vague, grumbling belly ache. Often people come to a reading so burdened in their minds that positive outcomes may not initially be viewed as being a

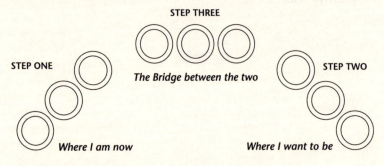

STEP THREE

The Bridge between the two

STEP ONE

STEP TWO

Where I am now

Where I want to be

Shores and Bridges

possibility. These cards will help release the disturbance by exposing its attributes through imagery and discussion.

The second step is for the friend to draw another three to six cards, which represent the shores she would like to arrive at for her greatest sense of well-being and recognition of her abilities. For example, 'Which career pathway will draw upon my talents and offer me satisfying challenges?'

The third step uses the image of a bridge, asking the question, 'What is the bridge between the shores on which I currently stand, and where I want to be?' This visual layout emphasises the possibility for finding pathways to creative changes. Again, the friend draws three to six images to represent the bridge.

It is an intuitive choice whether or not to draw all the cards and turn them up so the images are seen all at once, or whether to look at each question in sequence. I prefer to turn all the cards up, to absorb the overall picture and to see the various energies at play.

This three-step reading may be all the friend requires to bring about the beginnings of insight. Sometimes the cards do not fully mesh with the question asked. Then I ask the friend to pull a card — one for each card I am requiring clarification for.

At times, the reading will not give the ultimate clarity sought. This is not reason for despair. Ask for the next step. We are not always given the great unfolding of a vision at once. It may be a progressive process.

Read in communion with the friend. It is important, as the tarot reader, to remain centred in love, without attachment to the choices made by the friend. It is their journey — respect and trust the other will journey to the depths they are able to deal with and integrate.

Once the time to end the session draws near, I review and summarise the reading, recalling the significant interplay of energies and which directions have been revealed. The friend needs plenty of space, throughout the reading and on its completion, to talk about the relevance the symbols from the reading have in her own life and what the layout evokes for her. She may well have a very clear picture of the actions she will now take based on the sense of direction she has gained through seeing her life mirrored to her in the tarot spread.

The Traditional Celtic Cross Spread

The Celtic Cross spread is a much loved traditional tarot spread. With its many variations, it is probably one of the most useful and concise tarot layouts by which to reflect on any significant transition point in your life. The ten cards, each with their different focus of meaning, allow you to view your circumstances, options and attitudes from a variety of vantage points.

This layout, as with all tarot spreads, gives you symbolically a picture of your present experience. Your future is created through your responses to your current situation. Thus, the tarot spread awakens you to the degree of responsibility you are taking towards creating a future which will hold satisfaction and fulfilment for you.

Begin by finding your question. It is helpful to be specific, as you will then be able to utilise the interpretation of the image, knowing exactly the situation to which you are applying these symbols. Write down your question, and then begin to shuffle the cards. As you shuffle, maintain awareness of your question. Notice your breathing, and allow each breath to become full and relaxed.

When you are ready, lay the cards out in a fan, so that the back of each card is partially visible. You will be pulling ten cards, and placing them as depicted. Leave the cards face down until you have chosen all ten cards.

The first card represents the essence of yourself in the situation — the deepest motivating force.

The second card shows whatever is creating a disturbance, keeping you from the experience of fullness revealed in the first card. This may either be some personal doubt and disbelief which is undermining your intentions, or it may be a positive challenge, asking you to budge from a well-guarded position.

The third card portrays the thoughts you are most aware of,

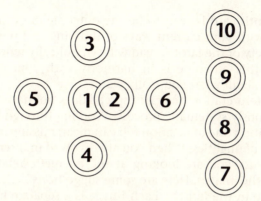

The Traditional Celtic Cross Spread

in relation to the question. This card often signifies logical thought patterns which have become stuck, creating a narrow view of the available choices.

The fourth card gives a message you need to see and hear more clearly. This card reminds you not to discount dreams, intuitive flashes and possibilities which are beyond your logical grasp.

The fifth card asks you to acknowledge whatever holds you back. See what needs to be released in order for you to move forward. This placement sometimes refers to past gifts and talents which need to again be drawn upon in order to bring wisdom and vitality to your present choices.

The sixth card represents what you are moving towards, or what you need to be open to encountering to make further progress.

The seventh card shows how your personality is responding to your circumstances. See if this image is a true face you are wearing, or a mask behind which you hide.

The eighth card represents the current environment around you. This may relate to a physical or an emotional atmosphere.

The ninth card portrays your hopes and fears in relation to your question. These may be intermingled as, often in the process of achieving something new for yourself, you will upset the old order of things.

The tenth card is seen to be the outcome of events if you proceed with your current ways of thinking and responding. The entirety of the tarot spread will symbolically reflect to you whether this outcome is in harmony with your conscious thoughts about what you really want.

The interpretation of a tarot spread does not have to follow any obviously systematic process. Working through the cards from position one to position ten can mean missing out on the interplay of qualities. When you are involved in interpreting a tarot spread, you are looking at the energetic relationships between the images. Here are some suggestions . . .

Breathe in the images. Each image is a separate ingredient which needs to be blended with the other nine images. Breathe them into your belly, as if your belly is a great cauldron. Feel the images swirling and mixing together, until you feel you have the taste — the flavour — of this reading.

As you are drawing the images together, be aware of the number of Life Songs in the layout and the relevance of the positions in which they are found. Life Songs are always present in a reading when significant transitions are taking place.

Be aware of the Shell Songs and their positions in the reading. These will indicate major roles which are to the fore, taken on either by yourself or by people who have influence in your life.

Notice the elemental balance of the Hearth Songs. Depending on the nature of your question, one elemental theme is likely to predominate. This preponderance will indicate whether the resolution to your question is to be found through exploring the realms of the feelings or of creative expression, or through enhanced mental clarity or by some very practical action.

Look for numerical links between the cards. For example, more than one First Song will indicate a bountiful time of new beginnings and blessings. More than one Tenth Song will signify a powerful time of completion.

Begin to voice the understanding you are receiving. Your thoughts do not have to be perfectly formed. Allow playfulness and humour to be woven into the reading, as it is through this relaxation that intuition and inspiration flow most easily.

If you have a suitable place, you may like to leave the images laid out, so you can continue to glance at them through the day. Sometimes it takes hours, days or weeks for the true relevance of the images to become clear. The purpose of using imagery is not to throw open the doors of the psyche willy-nilly but rather to gently, yet powerfully, coax out hidden self knowledge.

Always record your tarot spreads and the immediate responses you have. Leave space to add further comments, and to note the actual events which have occurred in relation to your question.

Shells, Masks and Shields

The Shell Songs are the focus of the following reading. Playing with these sixteen images gives us the opportunity to reflect on our roles, with their satisfactions and difficulties, and to see which new avenues we would like to explore. This spread is based on the first six placements in the Celtic Cross layout.

Firstly, take the sixteen Shell Songs from the tarot deck. Place the rest of the deck to one side. Shuffle the sixteen cards and, at the same time, allow images of your life roles to swirl around inside you. Watch these images as an interested and enquiring observer, rather than creating judgments.

When you feel ready, lay the cards face down, fanning them out so that the back of each is partially visible. Pull out six cards, being mindful of the qualities each is to represent, and place them as depicted. Leave all the cards face down until the six cards have been chosen.

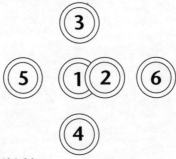

Shells, Masks and Shields

Each of these cards will give the answer to a question.

First card: 'What is the most significant role for you to focus on now?'

Second card: 'Which role is creating a sense of disturbance?' This may either be blocking the full expression of the first card, or it may be shaking things up and paving the way for change.

Third card: 'Which role do you have in full view right now, which is absorbing most of your conscious efforts?'

Fourth card: 'Which is the most important aspect of your inner life?' This may be a part of you which is hidden and protected by the third card, so that your sensitivity may develop in a place of safety.

Fifth card: 'Which role is passing out of your life?' This may be a role that once set you on your path and you are perhaps now ready to relinquish this to enable you to develop further.

Sixth card: 'Which role are you looking towards?' Envisage the expressive qualities which would align your inner life with the outer world.

Turn all the cards face upwards and reflect on the meaning they hold for you. Allow your intuition to speak to you before adding in the given interpretations from the book. Jot down the layout, and the thoughts which come to you.

If you require further clarification once you have completed the initial six-card spread, proceed as follows.

Remove the Life Songs from the deck you had placed to one side.

Shuffle these cards and spread them out, face down, in a fan. Look at each of the six cards in the spread, one by one, being aware of what role each represents. If you would like more information about the card's relevance, pull one of the Life Songs for each of the images which requires elucidation.

Seasons and Cycles

The following tarot spread is a very effective layout for portraying the diverse thoughts, feelings and reactions which often accompany a significant process of change.

To begin with, shuffle the cards and think about all the different aspects of the process of change you are experiencing. Spread the cards out in a fan, face down. Pull the cards you feel drawn to, placing them in the order depicted. With each card, focus on the essence the card signifies in the layout.

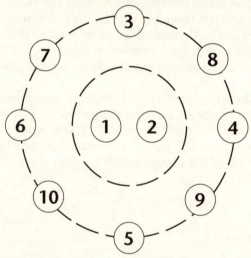

Seasons and Cycles

The first card — the Child Within — represents the naive, spontaneous, trusting view you have of the process you are in. This image may also signify the vulnerability and perhaps the hurt you are feeling.

The second card — the inner Wise One — represents the voice of your inner guide, giving you an overall perspective of where this change fits into the pattern of your life.

The third card — the Emerging theme — asks what new growth is finding its way to the surface of your conscious awareness.

The fourth card — the Manifesting theme — asks what has been brought to your full attention. What are you revealing to the world right now?

The fifth card — the Relinquishing theme — asks what you are having to let go of, or change your perspective about, in order to deal with these changes. Are you discovering hidden strengths you can draw upon?

The sixth card — the Transforming theme — asks if are you aware of acknowledging the endings as well as the beginnings. How are you marking this transition?

Cards seven, eight, nine and ten represent the awareness you need to move through this cycle of change.

The seventh card represents the awareness which will assist you in moving from endings into new beginnings.

The eighth card represents the awareness which will assist you in nurturing the budding new growth of your experience to fruition.

The ninth card represents the awareness which will assist you in expanding your perspective in order for your vision to flourish beyond your initial imaginings.

The tenth card represents the awareness of any energy-depleting patterns which hold you back from fully exploring your dreams.

Moon Gazing — Contemplating the Month Ahead

This tarot layout is an enjoyable way of combining ritual, tarot and the lunar pathways throughout our lives.

First find a calendar which marks the phases of the moon. It is most useful to begin working with this tarot spread during the dark phase of the moon or on the night of the new moon.

Draw the phases of the moon and mark in the dates for these in the month ahead.

| New Moon | Waxing Moon | Full Moon | Waning Moon | Dark Moon |

Moon Gazing — contemplating the month ahead

The New Moon — seeds of inspiration which have been nurtured in the dark, damp, warm soil of your creative imagination now become visible.

The Waxing Moon — this is the time to provide the climate in which your creativity can flourish. Courage, trust and determination will assist in the manifesting of your dreams and ideas.

The Full Moon — the potential hinted at in the New Moon is now ripe. Hidden thoughts and passions are revealed. New insights and a sense of clarity allow you to see your choices as opportunities to express your expansive and diverse nature.

The Waning Moon — completion and evaluation are vital processes which can be seen as psychic compost making. In this way there is no cutting off from past experiences but, rather, allowing the processes of transformation to work their magic.

Past learning experiences, no matter how they are initially judged, become future sources of wisdom.

The Dark Moon — a deepening of relinquishing and transforming occurs now. Your dreams may be full of rich symbols and you draw guidance from your intuitive knowing. It is important to ensure you set aside times for reflection, as the choices you make now pave the way for the new month ahead.

Jot down under each phase the plans you already have for this coming lunar month. If you menstruate, mark in when you are next likely to bleed. Tuning into this lunar cycle, shuffle the tarot cards and spread them out in a fan, face downwards. Pull a card, or cards, for each of these phases. See what messages of guidance the images have for you and see how these relate to the plans you have made. Are there any symbols indicating a need for greater flexibility? For more effort? For more time out and relaxation? For giving? For receiving?

By keeping a record and referring to these lunar readings you will move into a strong sense of the ebbing, flowing, waxing, waning, energetic tides in your own Being. You will also see the relevance the tarot archetypes have in your own experience.

To contact Catherine Cook and Dwariko von Sommaruga for information on ordering *Songs for the Journey Home*, and for workshop details, please write to Alchemists & Artists, PO Box 32 305, Devonport, Auckland, New Zealand.